*Free
the Child
in You*

Free
the Child
in You

*Take an Adventure
into Joyful Living
Through
Transactional Analysis*

JOHN K. BONTRAGER

A Pilgrim Press Book
from United Church Press
Philadelphia

Library of Congress Cataloging in Publication Data
Bontrager, John Kenneth.
    Free the child in you.

    "A Pilgrim Press book."
    Bibliography: p.
    1. Christian life—1960–   2. Transactional
analysis. I. Title.
BV4501.2.B62   248'.4   73-22120
ISBN 0-8298-0272-X

The scripture quotations are from the *Revised Standard Version of
the Bible*, copyright 1946 and 1952 by the Division of Christian
Education, National Council of Churches, and are used by
permission.

United Church Press, 1505 Race Street,
Philadelphia, Pennsylvania 19102

Dedicated to
Charles *and* Marguerite
who gave me life,
and to Vestal
who helped me to Free my Child
so that I could enjoy living

Contents

PART IV
Epilog 185

Illustrations

Foreword

If we consider the recent history of counseling and therapeutic modalities in this century, we can discern a basic trend: a gradual shift of emphasis from what goes on within a person—his individual thoughts and feelings—to what goes on between people—interactions and responses. At first, the psychoanalytic theory and method of Sigmund Freud built an *intra*-personal approach into the foundations of modern psychiatry; a person's early life experiences in great detail served as the therapeutic focus. Since then, as different schools of psychiatric thought have proliferated and evolved, an *inter*-personal approach has developed, expressing itself in such therapeutic modalities as the therapy group, the encounter group, family therapy and psychodrama. Perhaps the most popular mode, certainly the most widely known, is Transactional Analysis (T.A.), founded primarily by Eric Berne, M.D.

Practitioners of T.A.—most notably Berne, Thomas Harris and Claude Steiner—cite as advantages its simplicity and straightforwardness, its appeal, and its ready accessibility. The basic concepts—scripts; "strokes"; Adult, Parent, Child; trading stamps; Games like "Kick Me," "Schlemiel," and "Now I've Got You, You Son of a Bitch"—seem to awaken instant recognition in the many readers of the several best-selling books on the subject.

Given the growing popularity of the T.A. movement among laymen as well as therapists and counselors, this book is especially timely. Its author, Chaplain John Bontrager, is no mere abstract theoretician; he is a counselor with twenty years of clinical experience in work with individuals, couples, and families in distress. Influenced by and trained in the T.A. approach, he has put it to work for him in his pastoral counseling with marked success. But in this book he has taken the next daring and original step: he has used the idiom of transactional analysis to reinterpret Christian religious life. Not limiting himself to human behavior in Christian terms, he has used T.A. as the lens through which to view godhead itself.

One can readily anticipate that such an attempted wedding of T.A. and theology would prove a controversial one, the more so because Bontrager does not hesitate to challenge his fellow clergymen (as well as his lay readers) to scrutinize the validity of their work-styles, play-styles, and life-styles. He indicts as joyless a variety of aspects of Christian living from liturgical practice to pseudorecreational sports; from husband-wife relations to the relationship between man and his God.

Drawing on scripture, on the drug culture's tenets, and on his own extensive pastoral experience with contemporary religious and lay practice, Bontrager has synthesized a comprehensive document that is at the same time a sermon from scripture and a sound practical instruction in human relations; an exhortation to laymen and a challenge to the church. In clear contemporary language, speaking with the Natural Child's uninhibited enthusiasm, he has enunciated a joyous litany of liberation. It is a necessary work.

Thomas G. Gutheil, M.D.
Chief, Neuropsychiatry,
Naval Submarine Medical Center
Submarine Base, Groton, Connecticut

Preface

"Is this all there is to life?" This question has been asked by persons of all ages. The elderly man who has raised his family, worked hard all his life, and now in retirement waits from day to day to be released by death. The young mother who feverishly tries to keep ahead of the piles of clothes, dishes, runny noses, endless installment payments. The executive who feels the pressure of having to produce or else, afraid that something or someone will sabotage his image. The professional who is so concerned about being successful in his calling that he becomes a victim of the calendar and clock. Even persons in the religious establishment lose the bubble in finding real meaning in life. And the young person looks at all of this and promises himself he will not waste his life in this rat race.

Living is seen as a gigantic treadmill of activity, grinding away, but grinding up people in the process. What is needed is someone or something to put the pieces of life back together, to put the fragrance back in the flowers, the stars back into the sky, the intimacy back into relationships, the ability to touch, taste, smell, hear, see, and wonder.

We have the technology that permits us to walk on the moon, but our need is to be able to walk with another. We have computers that solve intricate problems in the blinking of an eye, but we find it difficult to share our innermost feelings with another. Our environment is filled with the wonders of electronics, yet we have lost touch with the unseen world of beauty, truth, and happiness.

Our communities have churches, synagogs, and temples of all sorts, yet the joy and creativity of religious faith seem to have vanished. Religion is often practiced as dogma and ritual; relationships are endured as necessities and life is boring.

In the opinion of the writer what is needed is a liberation movement. Crusades grow out of needs and the need has never been greater for the ability to enjoy life through the person of the Child. "Free the Child in you" is our slogan.

Wouldn't it be wonderful to recapture the imagination and wonder of the Natural Child? To feel once again the spontaneity, creativity, and excitement of life. To be able to explore and look and hear and taste and touch and smell. To be open to the world around you. To be able to waste a little time, turn off the clock, overcome hangups, to accept yourself as a worthwhile person. To appreciate the association with others. To drink from the satisfying waters of happiness, joy, and satisfaction.

Sometimes I am asked what racket I am in when people see the cross insignia on my sleeve. The answer may be given that the symbol is a telephone pole and that I am a communications technician. The cross *is* a special symbol to Christians. But as a clergyman my calling is communications—preaching, teaching, praying, liturgizing, counseling. I have the opportunity and responsibility also of helping others to be more effective communicators with man and God.

The person and teaching of Jesus have been grossly misinterpreted and misunderstood. Jesus has a life style which projects value and optimism into every person, every situation. His real enemies of the first century and this century are not those who claim to be atheists, but those who profess belief in God, their conception of God being that of an angry Deity who must be feared and appeased at any cost. Sin, imperfection, disobedience are emphasized by these persons who misrepresent the Christian faith. Ways of getting right and keeping right with God are stressed. The Christian faith becomes embedded in the concrete of legalism and ritual, with grace (which is the beautiful love of God shared with humans) being dispensed, not by God, but by God's representatives who control the supply and distribution. This concrete is further strengthened with the steel reinforcing bars of man's rules and regulations that describe godliness in terms of denial of the body, and holiness as avoiding sensual pleasure. Rather than being a gift, grace is conceived as something a person deserves when all the requirements have been met. Jesus is further molded into the one who has designed the blueprints of the system and is chief engineer of the factory which holds the patent rights on salvation.

It matters little whether these rules are formulated by "committee" action or whether the top or bottom person in the pyramid of professional religionists codifies them. Whether they come ex cathedra or from a local fundamentalist pulpit, the effect is still the same. The end products come off the assembly line mass-produced as "model Christians." One definition of "model" is "a small imitation of the real thing." Rather than having small imitations, would it not be more satisfying to deal with reality? What is needed is a technique to help us to evaluate truth and to make application of the truth in daily living. The technique called "Transactional Analysis" is a helpful tool and can be used by all persons to have a more meaningful and effective life.

Transactional Analysis helps one understand himself and his relationships by identifying the various dimensions of personality. In every circumstance a person is offered the opportunity of relating in one of three manners. These are Parent, Adult, and Child. A traffic light brings out the sharp differences among these modes. The red light is the Parent who is the authoritarian and possesses an operating code which was learned before the individual went to public school. The green light represents the Child who is always ready to go places and do exciting things that bring pleasure. Between these two is the yellow light or the Adult who approaches life cautiously and deals with data and facts.

Although Transactional Analysis is a fairly recent discipline, its goals and fruits are seen not only in the primitive church but also in the life and teachings of Jesus. Life is valuable and human relationships are important. The individual is seen as responsible for the way he lives his life. When he wills to control his destiny by a logical and rational approach (The Adult) he is able to be in charge of the powerful motivating forces in his life (The Parent) sometimes choosing not to play a preprogramed tape (Script) when it is contrary to his reason and hurtful to his happiness (The Child).

The person chooses to incorporate techniques and resource materials that bring fulfillment. One of the resources that projects worth in himself and others and gives his reason and will direction and encouragement is a viable Christian faith. This faith needs to be constructed upon truth. The basis of the truth is Jesus of Nazareth, his teaching, his life, his love. Transactional Analysis may help us understand this truth and make application of it in our lives.

It is interesting to see that Jesus has a three-dimensional approach to life. He has a Parent, Adult, and Child. This should give us insights as well as hope. The reference in Mark 10:13ff. where the mothers and fathers were bringing little children to Jesus emphasizes all three dimensions. The scene is set: "And they were bringing children to him, that he might touch them; and the disciples rebuked them." Jesus came through as Parent: "But when Jesus saw it he was indignant, and said to them, 'Let the children come to me, do not hinder them; for to such belongs the kingdom of God.'" Probably his voice, gestures, choice of words, facial expression all pointed to Parent. It hit the Adapted Child in the disciples and they must have felt small and put down. Wouldn't it be great to have videotapes of the historical encounters of Jesus rather than the printed page of the Gospel? This way we could have the emotions recorded. With the present system we must add the emotion like water to modern-day dehydrated foods to prepare them for the table.

Then Jesus came through as Adult: "Truly, truly I say to you, whoever does not receive the kingdom of God *as a child* shall not enter it." (Italics added.)* When he said this he showed that he had regained control over the Parent. There was probably little or no emotion. These are data of the kingdom. The Adult dimensions of the disciples must have responded to Jesus.

Then he showed the disciples and the people what he meant. He, himself, became Child. Bending down Child to Child: "He took them in his arms and blessed them, laying his hands upon them." His Adult said to his Parent, "Be quiet. I want to be with the children." His Adult liberated his Child and the response was O.K. He saw himself as "OK" and even the little children as "OK." And he said to the disciples and others, "Truly, I say to you, whoever does not receive the kingdom of God *as a child* shall not enter it." This is the message of Jesus. This is a condition of the kingdom of God. This is the "liberation" of the Child.

Just as Jesus can be seen in the dimension of the Adult and Child, he sometimes comes through as Parent. Some of the difficult passages of the Gospel account can be better understood with this in mind. The cursing of the fig tree (Matthew 21:18–20), the cleansing of the temple (Matthew 21:12–13), the counsel with the Canaanite woman (Matthew 15:22–28), the denunciations upon the scribes and Pharisees (Matthew 23:1–36) are illustrations where the Parent of Jesus was in control.

* The Greek phrase "Hos Paidion," often translated "like a child" can also be translated "as a child." The latter form is in the language of Transactional Analysis.

These New Testament passages have been confusing to Christians. But they are there even though they seem to be contrary to the spirit of Jesus. Yet, let us remember that Jesus comes through as we do, sometimes as Parent, sometimes as Adult, sometimes as Child.

It is not difficult to find passages of scripture where Jesus comes through as Adult. Portions of the Sermon on the Mount are excellent examples of Jesus teaching Adult to Adult, as he taught the facts of the kingdom. But, to be in the proper frame of mind and heart to enter the kingdom of God, one must "Free the Child," and receive the kingdom of God as a Child.

Our rational side (Adult) can sort through the facts. Our knowledge of right and wrong (Parent) tells us what to seek and what to avoid. But our Natural Child must be freed to receive the gifts God wants to share with us. And it is through the Natural Child that we experience the genuine, Christian joy which the disciples of the first century experienced. This is the ingredient of life that is so lacking in either a Parent- or Adult-oriented Christian faith. It is joy that Jesus shares with persons of every century. For he said, "These things I have spoken to you, that my joy may be in you, and that your joy may be full (John 15:11)."

The miracles, the "signs of the kingdom," the parables, Easter, Pentecost, Christmas, Good Friday, Lent can be studied through the Adult and "observed" by the Parent, but they can only be really understood by the Child. For example, the Adult may turn to the prophecy and Gospel accounts of Christmas. All the "facts" of Christmas can be studied and evaluated. The Parent can be concerned with orthodoxy and doctrine and insist that traditions be religiously kept. "Keep Christ in Christmas" is one of the slogans of the Parent. But the real understanding of Christmas only comes to the Natural Child who is open, unprejudiced, filled with wonder, possessing a vivid imagination, and creativity. The Natural Child has an urge to know and experience. This dimension of life is receptive and spontaneous; it expects angels to sing and shepherds to respond; it has no hang-ups concerning stars guiding people and God choosing to enter human history in the form of a baby born of a young maiden. The Natural Child "understands" because the Natural Child is freed from the hang-ups of reason, sophistication, scientific proof, objectivity, and formality and can respond to God who wants to communicate with men. Reality testing can be helpful, but not at the expense of the Natural Child.

There is another side of the coin. A little person can possess negative features that grown people should not copy. These are selfishness, greed, pride, hurting, rudeness, demands, spoiledness, exhibitionism, and temper tantrums. These are the qualities of the Adapted or "NOT-OK" Child and have been well learned to get favored treatment. Jesus never tells us to become "childish." He tells us to receive the kingdom of God as a child, which can be explained as the Natural Child that possesses the necessary prerequisites for receiving the kingdom of God. This is the quality that is inherent in human life before it is manipulated or distorted by conniving people. Other sections of this book will illustrate how people crave a dimension of happiness and self-realization and some of the techniques that they use to counterfeit the desired feelings.

The purpose of this book is to identify a quality of life that is inherent in persons of all ages. *Free the Child in You* is an attempt to wed the Christian faith to the methodology of Transactional Analysis in order to find a fulfilling way of life. Transactional Analysis helps a person understand and apply the Christian faith.

I am deeply indebted to the Reverend Mrs. Muriel Marshall James, D. Ed., who first introduced me to Transactional Analysis; to the late Eric Berne, M.D., who was the originator and trailblazer of this exciting and helpful discipline and especially for his books *Transactional Analysis in Psychotherapy, Games People Play*, and *Sex in Human Loving*; to Thomas A. Harris, M.D. who in his book *I'm OK—You're OK* not only describes the four life-styles of "I'm Not OK—You're OK," "I'm Not OK—You're Not OK," "I'm OK—You're Not OK," and "I'm OK—You're OK," with far-reaching moral implications, but mainly for his monumental statement, "I believe the Adult's function in the religious experience is to block out the Parent in order that the Natural Child may awaken to its own worth and beauty as part of God's creation." *

I am also indebted to Claude Steiner, Ph.D., for his book *Games Alcoholics Play*; to John Killinger, Ph.D., Th.D., for his encouragement and guidance; to Thomas G. Gutheil, M.D., who read the manuscript in its entirety and made numerous and helpful comments in addition to writing the foreword to this book; to brother Navy Chaplains Connell J. Maguire, Stephen N. Jones, Bernard G. Filmyer, James M. McCain, Jr., Dudley C. Hathaway, Maurice C. Slattery, and Victor J. Ivers; Lee

* Thomas Harris, *I'm OK—You're OK* (New York: Harper & Row, 1969), p. 234.

C. Miller, M.D., Price M. Chenault, M.D., Raymond J. Trettel, M.D., John H. Baker, M.D., Commander Bobby L. Stephens, MSC, USN; to Mrs. George Scully for typing the manuscript and for her beneficial assistance; to Christine Rodock for her artwork; and to my friend and colleague James E. Stark, M.D., Commanding Officer of the U.S. Naval Submarine Medical Center.

The opinions or assertions contained within this book are the private ones of the writer and are not to be construed as official or reflecting the views of the Navy Department or the naval service at large.

John K. Bontrager

1

What Is the Child
and Why Does It Need
to Be Freed?

Getting Some Handles

In every situation a person comes through in one of three ways: as Parent, Adult, or Child. This is the language of Transactional Analysis, an effective method of understanding persons and relationships. At first this system sounds complicated and difficult, but actually it can be easily understood and used even by young children.

Transactional Analysis is a concrete way of getting handles on life. It helps a person gain insights about his motivations and his relationships (transactions). He is able to accept himself as a worthwhile and responsible person and thus plan and control his life. The past is briefly examined but the emphasis is upon the present and the future. The system is a helpful tool as a problem-solver but can be used in any situation to evaluate the facts and make logical decisions. Not only does it help a person learn from past relationships, but it also serves as a helpful resource to engage in the midst of any happening.

Transactional Analysis was conceived and delivered in the clinical atmosphere of psychiatry and psychology. The professionals who gave birth to this exciting discipline did so only after intensive training and labor in the disciplines of traditional approaches to mental health. The application of its principles gives help and hope to a wide spectrum of people. Skilled therapists have treated a variety of emotional malfunctions and restored health to the patient. What used to be labeled with the stigmata of frightening names and diagnoses (schizophrenia, paranoia, kleptomania, etc.) can now be accepted and understood by therapist and patient alike without these labels of fear and hopelessness.

The original T/A therapists were recruited from the fields of psychiatry and psychology. They used their training and experience to formulate a solid foundation upon which to build an effective aid to mental health. The value of the program was recognized by others in the helping ministry. Social workers, teachers, clergymen, judges, counselors, and others were quick to show interest in this technique. The door was opened to any who wanted to apply these principles to their calling.

The beauty of T/A is that everyone can develop skill in its application. Depending upon the severity of the problem and the native resources available to the person, an individual can master its techniques even by reading a book on the subject. When therapy is necessary, each session with the therapist or group session brings the person closer to the time when he will be able to stand alone and make his own evaluations and decisions, and be able to live with his efforts. From the time a person enters therapy it is only a matter of time before he can take charge and be in complete control of his present and future. The goal of T/A is for persons to be able to make responsible decisions based upon fact and then be willing to assume the consequences of these decisions.

The concept in T/A is that a person has three potential ways of revealing his personality. He is not three persons nor is he pretending to be three persons. He is one person who comes through in one of three ways. His facial expression, his tone of voice, his vocabulary, his mannerisms are keys to this facet of his person. He does not act "childish" or "parental." He is Child or Parent. He does not role play "adult." He is Adult. "Golly," "gee," "gee-whiz," "goody," "groovy," "should," "ought," "must" are examples of terminology the person may use. The Parent scolds and is judgmental; the Child looks for ways of having fun; the Adult manages facts and data.

Figure 1 is an attempt to symbolize the three-in-one person. Rather than being "two-faced" this person is "three-faced." Only one dimension can be seen at a time in real life. He can shift from one position to another quite readily, or get hung-up on a certain position. He may choose to ignore a position. He may wish it would die and be gone forever. But the potential is there and the dimension can be revealed if properly motivated. If he gets locked in one position he may

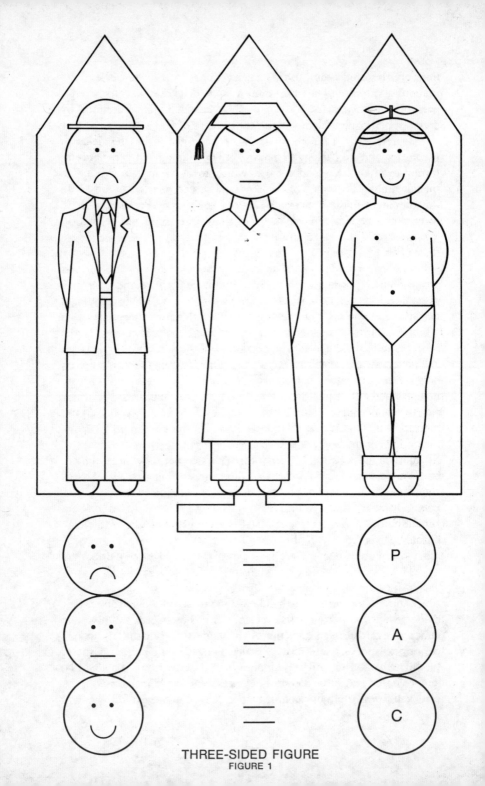

THREE-SIDED FIGURE
FIGURE 1

be a very sick person or a bore or a machine. T/A helps to identify the positions and to evaluate relationships.

The Parent

Every person has known authority figures who have left their imprint indelibly stamped on him. This dimension of life is called Parent for it resembles the way his parents (or those *in loco parentis*) looked at life and taught the little person to look at life. The imprint remains. It never grows dim. It is a controlling force when the person is three or seventy-three.

When the Parent is in control of the person, his statements, his opinions, his posture, his gestures, his tone of voice—all broadcast Parent. When little people play house and the roles of father and mother are assumed, it may be a shocking revelation when grownups overhear themselves mimicked by these little ones. This is an example of the Parent dimension and even small children have this dimension of life.

The authority figures have a powerful influence upon the lives of children. As with a hammer and chisel, the rules of life are carved into the character of the little person. This force becomes the basis of prejudice and affiliation. This influence is the foundation of conscience and the scales upon which right and wrong are weighed. This motivation is the rule book where good and bad are evaluated. It is as though father and mother are reincarnated in the offspring.

It has long been known that the early years of a person's life are important. It is during this time that the little person accepts and records from father and mother their views, rules, fears, anxieties, and hopes. This happens before the little person is able to filter out inconsistencies, contradictions of the facts. Everything is accepted as fact, at face value. Throughout his life his Parent speaks with authority and acts accordingly. The Parent lives there in his body as long as there is life in the body.

That every person has a dimension called Parent is a fact. Just as a baby cannot choose his father and mother so a person does not choose his Parent. It is there. It must be recognized and controlled. It is so much a part of the person that it is usually accepted as a very real part of his personality. A person may apologize for Parent-controlled decisions and emotions but he cannot rid himself of this facet of himself. This is not a role that is played. This is what a person experienced in his early relationship with authority figures. The Parent is what he learned about life and living from his father and mother. The information is unquestionably accepted as fact. It remains with the person all through life to guide him in his relationships.

The Parent dimension is seen as the "right" way of living. The rule book contains a vast amount of data which gives direction in many areas of life. This on-the-job training experienced in childhood motivates the person throughout his life. Table manners, prejudices, religious faith (or lack of it), morality, choosing a mate, diet, political affiliation, raising children, making a living, incurring financial obligations, paying bills, being a husband/wife/father/mother, cleaning house, maintaining and driving a car, recreation, handling emotions, playing Games, being an alcoholic, punctuality, dependability, honesty, laziness, getting along with people; all these are fibers accepted by the little person and woven into the fabric of his personality. This may be the truth that guides him in selecting his goals and living his life. This is his Parent and it is recorded within him for continuous replay in his future.

The Parent serves two useful functions. It is helpful in the rearing of children. It also gives rules and principles for living which makes certain routine decisions automatic rather than requiring the person to stop and think through an appropriate course of action. Thus much time is saved to be used in other ways.

THE CHILD

A second dimension of life is labeled the Child. Life is not just a blind acceptance of and following the rules. Emotions are involved. Just as a person had authority figures in his life, so he also had experiences which produced responses on the feeling level. These experiences are also permanently recorded. It is as though each person carries a little boy or girl on the inside to live and relive these experiences.

A baby records feelings long before he records rules or facts. It is believed that even before he is born he begins accumulating these data. He is powerfully affected by nonverbal communication. Long before he understands words he interprets tone of voice and stroking (or lack of stroking). He knows whether or not he is loved. He feels whether his environment is friendly. He decides whether life is worthwhile. He discovers ways of communicating and receiving recognition as a person. He learns effective techniques to control his environment. These may be by cooing, crying, smiling, laughing, temper tantrums, or conforming to expected behavior. He seeks rewards and avoids criticism. But he will be noticed, even if he has to experience pain to achieve recognition.

The world of the little person is discovered and lived through the senses. He hears, he tastes, he sees, he smells, he touches. He feels through the skin of his body and through his emotions. And he responds to these stimuli. Childhood is an exciting period. For the little person the world is filled with vast wonder and potential.

The emotional experiences are recorded by the little person before he leaves the home to begin his formal schooling. His personality is now shaped. His responses are now conditioned.

To understand the Child one must separate the Natural Child from the Adapted Child. The Natural Child is curious and receptive. He has urges to use his senses to explore his environment. There is an innate openness, trust, and spontaneity about him. He is not threatened by his dependence upon others yet he experiments with independence. He dreams, he wonders, he takes chances, he creates. He openly shows his emotions and reveals his motivations. He exposes himself. He is straightforward and unsophisticated. He is frank in his evaluation of self and others. He is free from hang-ups. He rebels against hypocrisy and sham. He admits mistakes without having to save face. He learns from his experiences.

The Natural Child is a fun-loving, sensuously motivated, happy person. He expects to find and does find happiness. He neither worries about the past nor fears the future. His world is the world of *now*. He lives in the present tense. His values have nothing to do with expense or effort. The smell of a flower or the softness of a kitten mean far more to him than chrome or wealth. He is unimpressed by titles, prominence, degrees, or honors. A mud puddle or sandbox to him has more potential than an expensive and complicated toy.

The Adapted Child is the polished product of demanding parents and society. He is pushed, bent, shaped, twisted, threatened into a conformist position by older persons who prepare him for the eventualities of life. The older generation seems compelled to pass on to the new generation the tools that will guarantee success in a competing environment. While discipline and leadership are necessary motivators to persons of all ages it is observed that these restrictions often hinder more than they help. Constricting techniques are often demanded by seniors of their juniors long after the real reason for using them has been forgotten. And in the above process the optimistic and exciting quality which is inherent in the Natural Child is smothered or seriously curtailed. A legalistic approach to rearing children is occasionally necessary. Punishment for disobedience is a requirement. But "Who makes the rules?" and "Are they really important?" need to be examined along with the degree and type of rewards and punishment offered. Playing in the street or playing with food on the plate are two different degrees of disobedience for a three-year-old. When a father spanks a son for any infraction of the rules his leadership is weakened. The little person becomes confused in his evaluation as to what is really important in life. Spanking needs to be reserved for potentially dangerous life and injury situations.

Mealtime in many homes is a painful experience. Instead of being a happy occasion for the breaking of bread and sharing of meaningful experiences, it becomes a ritualistic period to be endured. "Sit up at the table." "Don't spill your milk." "Don't play with your food." "Chew your food properly." "Don't talk with food in your mouth." "Don't put your arms on the table." "Clean your plate." "Use your napkin." "You'll sit at the table until you clean your plate." "Keep your plate in front of you." "Don't sniff at the table." Verbals and nonverbals are flashed from the authority figures. The table rituals that older persons learned in their childhood become dogma for the present generation. Variations of or disobedience to these sacred traditions are mortal sins to be avoided and punished quickly without mercy.

Having socially acceptable eating habits is a significant goal for concerned fathers and mothers, but they should never be at the expense of a painfully charged emotional atmosphere at mealtime. It is believed that the table can be an important clue to the evaluation of the Adapted Child. For the traditions of the past become the guides for the present. In addition, the frustrations of the father and mother are reenacted by harassing the children. It is not uncommon for parents to insist on the children following the rules while the parents openly violate them at the table. This contradiction is observed quickly by the children who consequently rebel and deliberately become disobedient to parental injunctions regardless of the punishment that follows.

To illustrate the Natural Child and the Adapted Child picture a mealtime situation where twin boys are personifications of these motivations. During the course of eating both of the boys burp loudly. The boy representing the Natural Child continues to eat, being unaware that he has broken any rules of etiquette or custom. His only concern is pleasure. He has the delight of relieving himself of gas and he continues to enjoy the delicious food before him. He neither glances to the right or to the left. He never misses a stroke of the fork nor stops chewing for a moment. The satisfaction of eating good and tasty food is his goal and he values every delicious mouthful. When he is full he will leave the table for other enjoyments, perhaps a nap, playing with friends, an ice cream sundae, or a movie.

The boy representing the Adapted Child is a much more complex unit. His motivation is to please others. He knows the rules and what is accepted behavior by other people's standards. He knows how to collect brownie stamps for good behavior.* He has learned when to speak and when to remain silent; he knows the "do's" and the "don'ts," as well as the consequences of each. He is most aware of nonverbal communications and has learned that a raised eyebrow or a sigh can have serious consequences. His motivation comes from authority figures outside of him (relatives, neighbors, clergymen, teachers, etc.) as well as the authority figure within him (his Parent). He must stay on the good side of both. He has learned to save brownie stamps. Everytime he does the right thing or refrains from doing the wrong thing he gets a brownie stamp to paste gleefully in his "brownie book."

When the Adapted Child accidently burps at the table his world comes to the end. The judgment day is present and he stands accused as guilty of a serious crime. He must make confession and do penance. He gets red in the face, immediately stops eating, apologizes profusely, asks if he should go to his room, begs for forgiveness, promises never to do it again, and then gets indigestion in the process. When he receives absolution he gleefully accepts his brownie stamp which he immediately pastes in his brownie stamp book. When the book is filled, he can redeem it for a valuable prize. The trophy reminds him of his obedience, fidelity, and valor.

---

* The concept of "trading stamps" is described in detail by the following authors: Eric Berne, *Principles of Group Treatment* (New York: Oxford University Press, 1966), pp. 286ff; Claude Steiner, *Games Alcoholics Play* (New York: Grove Press, 1971), pp. 16ff; Muriel James and Dorothy Jongeward, *Born to Win* (Reading, Mass.: Addison-Wesley Publishing Co., 1971), pp. 188ff. Many colors of trading stamps are used in TA to describe the motivation of the Adapted Child, viz., gray stamps—low self-esteem, red stamps—anger, brown stamps—inadequacy, gold stamps—self-appreciation, white stamps—self-righteousness, blue stamps—depression, etc. The color coding of ego stamp-saving is not the important issue. The motivation to collect stamps and thus "deserve" something is of concern for a person evaluating transactions. The goal of TA is to be aware of stamp collecting and to limit the need for stamps except for a few "gold" stamps. This book uses a general term "brownie" stamp to refer to trading stamps, especially as they apply to religious practice.

Another illustration of the Adapted Child is the man who accumulates brownie stamps over a period of time and when his book is full he redeems it for something he really wants and "deserves." This man takes out the garbage, mows the lawn, occasionally bathes the children, goes to church, washes the dishes, makes grocery runs, baby-sits the children, attends a boy or girl scout function, goes to a PTA meeting, etc., and when his book is full of brownie stamps he redeems it by staying out until four o'clock in the morning with the boys having a ball, wasting family money, getting drunk and making lots of noise. If you would ask him about this strange behavior he would tell you that he earned or deserved it, and that his pleasure cannot be denied.

Is this any different from the pious Christian who obeys all the rules day by day, spends his time collecting brownie stamps, and when his book is full he redeems it for the grandest of all prizes, which is "heaven"? When heaven's prerequisites are seen to be doing the good and refraining from the "no-no's," man becomes the Adapted Child who is pleasing some Parent, either within or without. This is a far cry from the "Good News" as taught and lived by the carpenter of Nazareth in the first century.

THE ADULT

The third side of the triangle of personality is labeled the Adult. The function of this important facet of life is to evaluate facts, make decisions, follow the decisions through to their consequences, and supervise the activities of the Parent and the Child. Unlike the Parent and the Adapted Child, the Adult makes a voluntary and conscious effort to control its destiny. It also assumes responsibility for its decisions. The Parent and Adapted Child are forced from the outside. The Adult comes from within.

The Adult is a computer. It sorts through the vast assortment of data. It examines each piece without emotion and without prejudice. It is completely objective and even its decisions are reprogramed constantly for evaluation when new data are available. The Parent and Child are both charged with feeling but the Adult stays calm and collected in any situation, as long as it maintains control. The Adult evaluates the rules of the Parent and the emotions of the Child and tries to keep them appropriate to the other data.

The Adult (as well as the Parent and Child) is standard equipment for every person. Even a little person has an Adult. The mentally retarded or mentally ill person also has an Adult. Each person has a computer. The function of each computer is to manage data. Not all, however, are endowed with computers of equal ability. Some are able to handle more complex problems than others. The design and function are equal. But the quality and volume vary from one person to another.

Life would be complex but drab if a person had only an Adult dimension (without a Child or Parent). This person, if his existence were possible, would be interested only in facts. No one ever marries a computer. No one would want to eat breakfast with a computer. No one would want a computer to be the mother of his children. No one would take a computer to a party as his companion. The ability to spit out facts unemotionally would not be a good credential for a friend, companion, or lover. The Adult does not exist by itself. It needs the Parent and the Child just as they need the Adult. The Adult needs to be in charge, monitoring the emotions of the Child and the rules of the Parent. When the Adult maintains control, realistic goals are formulated and reached, life is fulfilling, relationships are mutually beneficial, and humanity profits from the contributions that are made.

Decisions can be made along any of the three dimensions. A person's signature on a contract is written there by one of the dimensions. If decisions are made by the Adult dimension after considering all the facts, then likely the individual will be able to live with the decision. But if it is made by either the Parent ("This is what you should/must do") or the Child ("Golly, wouldn't it be fun to do that?") without consulting the Adult, sticking to the decision will be more difficult.

What dimension is a person in when he goes shopping for an automobile? If his Adult is in control, he will look for a dependable car, with an efficient engine, low cost, high resale, low depreciation. He will be unimpressed with luxury equipment like stereo tape decks, air conditioning, and lots of chrome. He will look for dependable transportation that will give him durable and economical service. If the Parent is in control he will look for a car, just like the kind Dad used to buy, a certain make, model, and body style. It is as though Dad goes shopping for him and the car he notices and buys pleases the Parent figure in him. The Child dimension is most impressed with speed, sound, color, shine, peer approval, and pickup. The cost, how much and how long the monthly payments extend are of little importance. He wants his pleasure now and he wants it big. He is willing to sign on the dotted line right now if he can have immediate delivery.

Being able to identify these three dimensions in self and others gives insights and understanding. Keeping them appropriate according to the situation helps give a rewarding and meaningful life.

2

The Transaction
and Programing

THE TRANSACTION

The interaction between two or more persons can be described as a transaction. The science that analyzes the resulting communication or lack of communication is called Transactional Analysis. Any situation where people interact can be recorded in a simple diagram. This ability to record and interpret a transaction makes the person a specialist in Transactional Analysis. This technique can be understood and used by any person who takes a few minutes to learn some very simple terminology and concepts. The purpose of this chapter is to explain this system and perhaps whet the appetite of the reader so he will want to turn to the works of other writers in this field who go into greater detail on the subject.*

In each situation a person may come through as Parent, Adult, or Child. The person receiving the transactional stimulus may "hear" the communication through the ears of his Parent, Child, or Adult. Figure 2 shows a typical communication between the Adult of two persons. The conversation dealing with facts is sent and received Adult to Adult without emotion. Person X states (1), "It is raining outside." Person Y responds (1), "I know. I can hear the rain beating against the window."

* Books by Eric Berne, Thomas Harris, Claude Steiner, Muriel James and Dorothy Jonegeward as listed in the Bibliography.

No one gets up tight since no one is threatened. The transaction will continue until the two persons separate. During the conversation the topic may be shifted occasionally but as long as the Adult of each person is in control the stimulus and response will be complementary and communication is likely to result. If at any point one or both of the parties becomes emotional then it is known that the individual has shifted from the Adult position to either the Parent or to the Child.

In Transactional Analysis a necessary point to be kept in mind is that it is important to deal, not only with what is said, but also with what the other person "hears" and reacts to. Being aware of nonverbal communication is also extremely important as this may validate or invalidate what a person says with his mouth.

Figure 2 also shows the husband making the statement to his wife on the Adult to Adult level. Verbally he says, "Are we having stew again for supper?" But the dotted line from Parent to Child shows the real message to be something quite different. The nonverbals (tone of voice, gestures, facial expression, sarcasm) say, "You are stupid, dull, and inadequate. You will always be an inferior cook and wife." The wife is likely to respond in one of three ways. She may respond Adult to Adult, "Yes we are having stew but we are also having German chocolate cake for dessert and I know how you like cake."

She may respond Child to Parent, "I know I am not a good cook and I will never be able to prepare meals like your mother." She may squeeze a tear or two and go charging off to lock herself in the bedroom where she cries for two hours.

A third likely alternative is for the wife to have some accumulated "emotional garbage" inside and when she is criticized she must return in kind and dump her "garbage" all over her husband. Thus she may respond with, "You stingy penny pincher. If you weren't such a stupid pig you would make more money and I could buy some decent food for a change." Responding as Parent to Child she will probably show great emotion and is likely to flash some red-hot nonverbals as well.

A simple illustration shows what actually happens when there is a difference between what is said and what is understood. Can you imagine a man bouncing Ping Pong balls across the table to his wife on the other side? She may catch the balls and toss them back to him. Both are aware of the Ping Pong balls and both are involved in catching and tossing the balls. This is symbolic of Adult to Adult transactions. Everything is "above board." What is openly communicated is

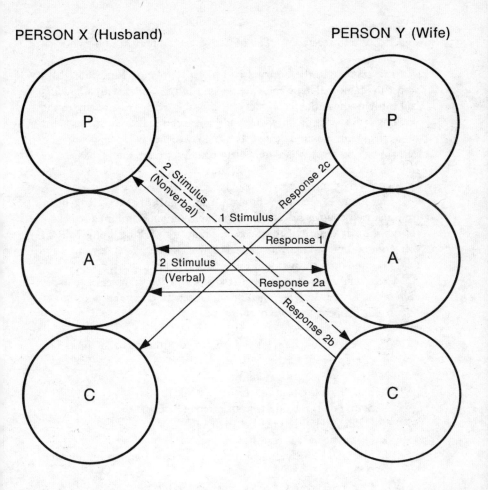

PERSON X (Husband)   PERSON Y (Wife)

1.   Stimulus   "It is raining outside."
1.   Response   "I know; I can hear the rain beating against the window."
2.   Stimulus (*verbal*)   "Are we having stew again for supper?"
2.   Stimulus (*nonverbal*)   "You are stupid, dull . . ."
2a. Response   "Yes, we are having stew but we are also . . ."
2b. Response   "I know that I am not a good cook and I never . . ."
2c. Response   "You stingy penny pincher. If it weren't for you . . ."

TRANSACTIONS
FIGURE 2

understood and reacted to in an objective way. There are no emotional overtones.

But suppose as the husband is involved in tossing Ping Pong balls across the table suddenly the wife gets hit in the ankles with a bowling ball thrown under the table. She will probably react emotionally to the bowling ball that brought shock and pain to her. This illustrates what nonverbals can communicate. These may belie what is being said verbally and may cause an immediate reaction in the wife. Chances are she will toss a bowling ball over the table or more than likely she will hit him with something else more openly.

This figure of speech has brought many smiles of acknowledgement from married couples searching for better communication in a marriage relationship. It describes the need to be aware of Ping Pong balls in conversation but also to be able to recognize and deal with bowling balls that are sometimes thrown under the table.

Communication results when the lines in the transaction parallel each other. However, when the lines intersect the communication stops. When this happens the two people may:

1. Make accusations, use loud voices, threats and profanity (Parent).
2. Resort to violence (Child).
3. Flee from the painful situation (Child).
4. Stare down the one who threatens (Parent).
5. Deliberately keep quiet (Adult).
6. Drink alcohol, ingest drugs (Child).
7. Blackmail, including threatened suicide, homicide, divorce (Child).
8. Cry, pout, throw temper tantrums (Child).
9. Get reinforcements (Child).
10. Objectively evaluate the transaction and laugh at one's ridiculous behavior (Adult).

The great value of Transactional Analysis is the handle it provides to enable a person to objectively evaluate transactions and be able to see some humor in the relationship. This does not mean that a person laughs at another for that would be threatening and painful. But to see the absurdity of a situation, particularly as it regards the self, and to be able to laugh at yourself is a great asset and tension reliever. It is hard to be angry and threatened by someone who begins laughing at his own shortcomings and uptightness. This kind of laughter usually brings a complementary reaction in the other person.

The ability to see humor in a tense situation can come only when the Adult is able to evaluate objectively the absurdity of an uptight transaction and to see and hear how ridiculous the demands of the Child or the Parent actually can be. The ability to recognize humor when one's Child or Parent has made heavy demands is a sign that growth is taking place. One of the greatest compliments a wife can make of her husband's growth, for instance, is for her to say, "He can now laugh at his Parent, whereas before he always took his Parent so seriously." What she really is saying is that her husband now is usually able to keep his Adult in control of his Parent and that he can effectively evaluate the demands of the Parent when the Adult has momentarily lost control.

The Parent-Parent or Child-Child transaction needs to be examined briefly. Parent-Parent discussions rarely solve problems. Being able later to evaluate the data generated from a Parent-Parent dialogue when the Adult is in control can be of some benefit. But at the time a Parent-Parent dialogue is usually a statement of positions with no desire to seek feedback or new ideas.* There is a lot of talking, little listening, and very little thinking. It is as though two persons activate prerecorded tape recorders and leave the room as they play without supervision.

A visit to the Chief Petty Officer's Club or Master Sergeant's Club will give plenty of illustrations as to what takes place when conversations occur Parent-Parent. A favorite topic is the shortcomings and inadequacies of men newly recruited, or that the Navy/Army/Air Force/Marine Corps/Coast Guard is not what it used to be. If the conversations of husband and wife are generally on a Parent-Parent level, much talk will be made with little learning, and very little helpful action resulting. Parent-Parent transactions structure time, but like many PTA meetings the reading of the minutes of past meetings will generate little enthusiasm and be of marginal value.

The Child-Child transaction is much more fun. Here the guideline is something that is mutually pleasurable, to be done just for the fun of doing it.

Sexual relations at their best are Child-Child. Even the prelude to sexual intercourse carries the designation "foreplay." Without love (which includes respect, tenderness, responsibility, unselfishness, open-

---

* Dr. Berne describes Games and Pastimes played at the Parent-Parent level. *Games People Play* (New York: Grove Press, 1964), "PTA—Projective Type," p. 43 and "Ain't It Awful" (Nowadays), pp. 110ff are illustrations of this type.

ness, fondness, receptivity), sexual intercourse is mechanical, selfish, sometimes degrading—mutual masturbation. Sexual relations at their best are a special way of communicating love through verbal and nonverbal symbols in a marriage relationship. Fear of discovery, possible unwanted pregnancy, venereal disease, loss of reputation, rejection by mate—all put premarital and extramarital sexual relations in serious question. Two people promising to assume the responsibilities of intimate living with its legal ramifications will want to be responsible for and to protect their relationship and resulting offspring with every legal, moral and spiritual blessing.

The Adult dimension sets the scene for lovemaking. For this reason when two married persons in love go to bed for reasons other than sleeping they probably do so behind a locked door. Even the telephone connection to the outside world usually is inactivated. In the privacy of the bedroom the two seek new ways of bringing happiness and joy to one another. They maintain an atmosphere of respect and joy, avoiding pain and giving only pleasure. The Adult of each supervises the Child and keeps the responses appropriate. The Adult-Adult relationship later gives counsel and understanding when there are any hangups or tension in the sexual relationship.

Parent is judgmental and demanding; Adult is objective and unemotional; Child is uninhibited and sensuous. Sex at its best is Child-Child, where pleasure is given and received just for the sheer fun of doing it. The orgasm is the bonus that comes out of this relationship.

In the venture of rearing children the Parent in the father and mother is stimulated. The children's activities must be supervised. Their future must be planned. Mothers and fathers must make decisions that affect their offspring until the Adult of the little person can function on its own. Revised decisions may be made at a later date by the Adult of the children. A most important point is that the Adult must always supervise the Parent and the Child. The Adult observes the administration of the punishment of the Parent and makes certain it is appropriate and understood. The Adult sets the scene for the Child and gives permission as needed. For instance, a couple may have a marriage certificate hanging on their bedroom wall showing their sexual relationships are legal, moral, and spiritual. But the Adult says, "Do not have sexual intercourse on the front lawn." "Lock your bedroom door." "Pull down the shades." "Take the phone off the hook." "It's OK to experiment with new techniques and positions in lovemaking." "Don't bring pain to your mate." "Don't give hang-ups to your mate." The

Adult is the supervisor that keeps life and emotions appropriate for the occasion.

The "I'M OK—YOU'RE OK" husband or wife brings to that marriage bed or marriage discussion the most helpful and fruitful tools and raw material. Their lives are secure and they are secure in the presence of others. They need not be threatened by forces outside or within the home.

The ability to apply these data to a person's life can give many insights which result in a whole new outlook on relationships. It can help a person confront his life-style and change to the "I'M OK— YOU'RE OK" position. It can help a person look behind some of the choices he has made in the past. For instance, the author is always fascinated when two persons present themselves to be married. Sometimes the question is asked, "Why did you pick him/her?" The question usually gets some foggy responses like, "Because I love him" or "Because I just want to marry her." Here is an attractive and promising young lady. Obviously she has been noticed by a myriad of boys and young men as she went to school and participated in a variety of social activities. She probably dated a number of young men during her courtship period. She has obviously had many proposals for marriage. What was she looking for? A tall one, short one, skinny, athletic, a blonde, brunette; blue eyes, long arms, a brain; a charmer, a flatterer; hairy, manly, clever? Did she have a check-off list of desirable qualities and, up until she met her one-and-only, was she only "window shopping?"

And the young man. Why did he pick her? What was *he* looking for? What were *his* standards? To get a girl "Just like the girl that married dear old Dad"? Was he secretly looking for a mother substitute, a carbon copy, an ideal, a perfectionist, an angel, a "baby" to care for? Did he decide on "second best"? Was he content with what nobody else wanted?

Before the days of Transactional Analysis the writer would have settled for a pat answer to this question. Now after years of testing and evaluating feedback I suggest that a person marries out of his need. He looks for a person that helps to fulfill this need. It is suggested that a girl with a strong Parent will be attracted to, and will probably marry, a young man with a strong Child. She feels comfortable with him. She knows and understands him. She feels needed by him and has something to offer him. I propose that a young man with a strong Child will seek out a mate that will meet his Child needs. He needs a housekeeper. He needs someone who will look out for him, make his decisions for him, wash his socks, pick up his clothes, remind him of his appointments, get him to his job on time, select his clothes, pay his bills, send out his Christmas cards, remember anniversaries, and nag him a little. He needs someone who will provide an environment for him to continue to be irresponsible, selfish, and undisciplined. He wants her to complain, to scold. He needs her "mothering." If she were to change after marriage without his desiring to change, he would be frustrated and insecure. If after marriage she would refuse to fill this role and come through as strong Child or more threatening yet, strong Adult, his position would be unbearable. It is suspected that his life position is still "I'M NOT OK—YOU'RE OK" just as it was when Momma stroked him in the crib. Perhaps his wife's life style is "I'M OK—YOU'RE NOT OK" and so their relationship is complemented. But suppose, for some reason, she moves to the "I'M OK—YOU'RE OK" position and becomes unwilling to play his childlike Game of "Take care of me." A couple who has reached this point can profit greatly from the insights of Transactional Analysis.

This matter is further complicated in that during courtship persons are usually on their best behavior. They try to camouflage their true position and it may not be known until some months after marriage that both are strong Parent and weak Adult and Child. Underneath the patched jeans and bare feet is revealed the position "I'M OK—YOU'RE NOT OK." What is ahead for this couple who finds that one in the marriage feels "I'M OK—YOU'RE NOT OK"? Can anything be done after marriage to cure incompatibility and conflict? Can anything really help these "NOT OK" people?

Premarriage counseling should revolve around mastering the techniques of Transactional Analysis. A couple has a running start for happiness and Game-free living if they can speak this language in their relationship. These premarriage sessions would be on the Adult-Adult level which is nonthreatening and conducive to learning. What a far cry from the older approach of a clergyman (Parent) giving marriage "advice" to the couple (Child)! Clergymen have to labor diligently to free themselves from coming through as Parent. The pulpit, the altar, the confessional, the training, the calling all encourage the clergyman to come through as "Father" which is Parent. Besides, it is satisfying and comfortable to be set apart from the people by being a "man of the cloth," meaning "some special breed of person." To be able to come down from the holy mountain and share with people what God has revealed, what he expects of the faithful, and how they can get the goodies of heaven gives the clergy an aura of authority. To intercede on parishioners' behalf at the altar or in some other sacramental dispensation further encourages the clergy to overestimate their value. Being unable to distinguish between the man and the man of God causes many a promising clergyman to become just a pompous ass in and outside the temple.

It is much more painful and demanding to live and work and breathe with people. To share their hopes, fears sufferings, and joys. Pat answers and advice, no matter how brilliant, are just not helpful. The "I'M OK—YOU'RE NOT OK" clergyman will come through as Parent in the pulpit, study, and home. He has all the answers but he probably does not understand the questions. His Parent scolds, pleads, threatens, whines, directs. He becomes God's angry man who must force-feed the people who do not know what's good for them. Besides this, his Parent assures him that when he speaks it is really God speaking. He forgets, however, that the direction of the Holy Spirit is the evidence of the presence and voice of God. He uses his position, the Bible, ecclesiastical pressure, and religious law to reinforce his Parent.

This type of clergyman personifies the scribes and Pharisees of the New Testament more than the One who called and ordained him. The Master Teacher shared life intimately, not only with twelve men, but with all who felt comfortable around him. His ability to establish rapport with people and consequently to have an effective ministry was his ability to refrain from coming through as strong Parent. He rarely scolded or threatened. The occasions recorded where he raised his voice or when his Adult lost control can be counted on one hand. Persons who describe him as either pious or harmless do him and his cause a great disservice. His position was neither judgmental nor detached. He was not a rule-giver nor a meek and mild "Milquetoast." When he was in a group others felt his presence, not because he made loud demands but because he had a genuine concern to know and share in meeting the needs of people. He lived "I'M OK—YOU'RE OK," and persons were drawn to him and influenced to reflect the same life-style. From this life position he was at home with the people in the temple, in the home, in the fields, on the street, and at social events. His "I'M OK—YOU'RE OK" style was unthreatened by accusations of being a winebibber or associating with "inferior" or "unclean" people.

One area where crossed transactions are painfully apparent is in the so-called generation gap. The crossed transactions make the gap wider and hold people apart. The breakdown in communication between persons in and out of related generations proceeds from an "I'M OK—YOU'RE NOT OK" position. When the Parent or the Child calls the shots, communication deteriorates. The "I'M OK—YOU'RE NOT OK" of the Parent in one person confronts the "I'M OK—YOU'RE NOT OK" of the Child in the other person and a stalemate results. Both persons are threatened because both positions are insecure and inadequate.

The Over Thirty (O/T) position of "I'M OK—YOU'RE NOT OK" comes from the Parent being in control with the Adult running scared and the Child trussed up in the corner. The Under Thirty (U/T) position of "I'M OK—YOU'RE NOT OK" comes from the Natural Child being in command without the supervision of the Adult and lacking the discipline and the rulebook of the Parent. Both positions reach out for support and approval from kindred "minds." The O/T's muster reinforcement from others who are Parent-motivated. The U/T's band together with others who are Child-oriented. The battlelines are drawn.

In addition the O/T's emphasize the tenets of their faith that safeguard their world and make life meaningful (rules, discipline, status quo, future rewards, orderliness, neatness) while the U/T's react against these and openly flaunt their disregard for them. Both groups gain support by living their creed. The U/T's get a bonus, by having the pleasure from short-range goals but also irritating the hell out of the O/T's in the process. The O/T's also have a fringe benefit: Since they represent the power structure they gleefully pursue "witch hunts" and prosecutions of the recalcitrants.

Some of the ways that U/T's satisfy the Child with the additional benefit of irritating and threatening the Parent in the O/T's are as follows:

Long Hair
Careless dress
Irresponsibility
Money a means to an end, not an end
Loud and original music
Open sex
Carefree Child with the ability to play (Natural Child)
Desire for immediate satisfactions
Marijuana

Drug abuse
Rejection of traditional approach to religion
Loyalty to peers

The O/T's react to these qualities just about as a bull does to a red flag. Each item is a threat to the life position of the O/T's and a reminder of the disrespect and contempt of the U/T's.

Whenever communication is not supervised by the Adult it is very likely that Games will be played. The effort to isolate and dissect Games is a related field of Transactional Analysis. These Games differ from those played to pass the time and stimulate social intercourse in that these Games are not played for fun. They are played with great effort for a pathological reason—The Payoff. The goal of a Game is to manipulate people and situations and get a Payoff, usually at someone's expense. They are played by the Parent and the Child with the Adult assuming the stance of the three monkeys, hiding his eyes and his ears and his mouth. Even though the Games are usually unconsciously played, the choice of the Game and the moves that are made are done with the same seriousness as participants in a chess tournament. The same feeling of victory comes when a Game is concluded and the trophy is presented.

Games can be played by everyone. The "I'M OK—YOU'RE OK" person usually is conscious that he is involved in a Game and he knows how to break it up whenever he chooses. Persons who have the other life positions ("I'M NOT OK—YOU'RE OK," "I'M OK—YOU'RE NOT OK," and "I'M NOT OK—YOU'RE NOT OK") habitually play Games to their painful outcomes and accept the Payoff with great satisfaction and glee. Games are played in the kitchen, den, living room, dining room, bedroom, office, school, factory, aircraft carrier, military station, church, synagog, cocktail lounge, court room, legislature, clinic, farm back yard, patio, and ocean liner. They are played by clergymen, medical doctors, teachers, workers, soldiers, officers, dependents, sailors, husbands, wives, children, lawyers, politicians, artists, musicians, laborers, grocers, addicts, sportsmen, athletes, dancers, gardeners, housewives, and farmers. They are played by people until they die or choose not to play. The Adult is the one who must bring Game playing to an end.

Games are a substitute for intimacy. Those who must play Games are trying desperately to fill an emotional void. They do it by a series of skillful maneuvers to bring about a Payoff. They need the psychological victory and the feeling of being in control of themselves and others. They will continue to play Games until:

1. They die.
2. Others refuse to play.
3. They experience a feeling of intimacy.
4. They choose to strengthen the Adult and be controlled by the Adult.

A person who has his Adult in control may occasionally play a Game. But he may *choose* not to play. Those who permit their Parent or Child to be in control are likely candidates for a lifetime of Game-playing. They cannot choose to play or not to play. The Adult knows all about Games and about the Parent and Child. He also knows about the need for intimacy. And so he chooses the methods and transactions that bring him the greatest satisfaction.

The person desiring to end a Game and have a more intimate relationship must use his Adult to reach the Adult in the other person. If the other person refuses to move from either a Parent or Child position the Game will be postponed until he can find another partner. Husbands and wives often play Games whenever their relationship is fragile and they are unable to interact on an Adult to Adult level. If one desires to put his Adult in Control, end the Game, and achieve an intimate relationship, he must call the Game by its name and state that he refuses to play. If he has recently learned the handles of Transactional Analysis he may be able to share these with his mate, but only if the mate will respond with the Adult, since little satisfying learning takes place outside the Adult-to-Adult level. If the mate then puts the Adult in control, a wholly new and joyful relationship awaits this couple. If the mate refuses, the person whose Adult is in control has the following choices:

1. To wait until the mate can have the Adult in control.
2. To move to the Parent and interact as Parent-Child.
3. To return to the Game (or another Game).
4. To encourage the mate to receive T/A therapy.
5. To go to Child-Child and play in the bedroom-recreation room.
6. To get a divorce.
7. To become a martyr.

Little is accomplished unless the discussion is Adult-Adult. It is for this reason that it is hopeless to continue the discussion when one or both of the persons is emotional (Parent or Child).

Similarly, when a mate is under the influence of alcohol or drugs it is generally useless to have a discussion of issues and relationships, since that person is probably showing only the Child. When the mate is intoxicated the other person has the following choices:

1. Shift to the Parent and start complaining.
2. Shift to the Child and get drunk also.
3. Retreat for the moment (regroup).
4. Refuse to continue the discussion until both Adults can be in control.
5. Recognize that the mate may be playing a Game (Alcoholic) and refuse to play.
6. Later suggest Transactional Analysis therapy and insist that both receive the benefits from it.
7. Continue to play Games with each other.
8. Get a divorce.
9. Become a martyr.

Every clergyman has probably been called out of a deep sleep by a person who is intoxicated. Much pressure is made to have an immediate discussion of religion, problems, or issues. An inexperienced and naive counselor may reluctantly accept the challenge. But it is hopeless, since the Adult of the clergyman must deal with the Child of the counselee. Some counselors feel the experience may be a fruitful way of seeing the Child of the person, but little can come from the interview.

Appointments made on the telephone at 2 A.M. are rarely kept the next day. The clergyman will be a more effective counselor (and will have his sleep interrupted less) when he realizes that unless the interview is Adult-Adult, little constructive results come about in a counseling situation. In fact, it would be very easy for the counselor to come through as strong Parent if the Child is in control of the other person. He could play the role of prosecutor or rescuer from the Parent position and thus encourage the person to continue to play the Game "Alcoholic." *

* Eric Berne, *Games People Play* (New York: Grove Press, 1964), p. 73.

Programing

Dr. Thomas A. Harris, in his book *I'm OK—You're OK* gives a very helpful Analysis of the four life positions of Transactional Analysis and the resulting moral application. Dr. Harris writes:

> Very early in life every child concludes, "I'm not OK." He makes a conclusion about his parents, also: "You're OK." This is the first thing he figures out in his life-long attempt to make sense of himself and the world in which he lives. This position, "I'M not OK—You're OK," is the most deterministic decision of his life. It is permanently recorded and will influence everything he does. Because it is a decision it can be changed by a new decision. But not until it is understood.*

This evaluation of life by the baby is an emotional response to those who touch him during his infancy. A human baby is a helpless bundle of potential. Unattended he will die. In comparison with other mammals that can care for themselves soon after birth the baby is completely dependent upon seniors to feed, clothe, and protect him. The little one seems to sense this dependence and structures his outlook on life accordingly.

A person may be hung up on the life position "I'M NOT OK—YOU'RE OK." He may go through life expecting little or nothing from himself. He may never get over his intense feeling of inadequacy, content to live in the shadows of life, withdrawn from the arena where "OK" people interact. In the process he follows a life plan or script that enhances this position. He may be like the person who has a sign on his back saying, "Kick Me," only the person knows the sign is there and he unconsciously believes that he not only deserves to be harassed but that others have the right to do so. He needs the stroking that others can give even if it is achieved in a painful fashion.

Dr. Harris states that often this person will adapt a counterscript which fulfills the requirement "YOU CAN BE OK, IF." "Such a person seeks friends and associates who have a big Parent because he needs big strokes, and the bigger the Parent, the better the strokes." † His life is a series of efforts to try to earn the approval of others. But since the basic position is one of self—"NOT OK," life is a painful

---

* Thomas A. Harris, *I'm OK—You're OK* (New York: Harper & Row, 1969), p. 37.
† Ibid., p. 45.

series of realizations of inadequacy and unworthiness. The person has a need to experience a continuous reinforcement of his "NOT OK" position. He is "happy" when he is reassured that he is "NOT OK."

The second life position "I'M NOT OK—YOU'RE NOT OK" is adopted by the person who sees no value in himself or others. Rather than looking for good in himself and others he expects to find (and consequently finds) this life position reinforced. He says, "I'm worthless—You're worthless, and consequently living is worthless." This life script may program the person to attempt homicide and/or suicide.

The third life position is "I'M OK—YOU'RE NOT OK." This person values himself but sees no good in others. This is the feeling of self-righteousness with the inability to identify with anyone, since all others are unworthy. The person with this life script is motivated by his Parent with neither evaluation nor control by the Adult. He has no feeling for the rights and property of others. He feels that the world revolves around him and he deserves anything he wants. Whether it is at the expense of others is not even considered by him. His selfish and self-righteous outlook never considers the feelings and needs of others, since they are not OK. He is a bully, a deserving and hungry bully, and he stops at nothing to satisfy his needs. A person with this life script is cruel, assaulting, inconsiderate, and demanding. He is programed for homicide, and lawlessness of every description.

Happiness escapes the first three life positions. There is little permanent satisfaction in looking down on self or others. Depression, frustration, and despair are the companions who walk the sidewalks of superiority or inferiority.

Feelings that motivated the infant to adapt an inadequate life position cannot be erased. Every person, including a baby, has a great need for stroking. However, when maturity comes and the Adult is strengthened, the tape which once programed an unhealthy response to self and others can be evaluated and if need be, it can be forsaken and a more healthy one embraced.

A goal of Transactional Analysis (and also the Christian faith) is to enable persons to have an "I'M OK—YOU'RE OK" position. A realistic approach to life which sees good inside and out, worth in self and worth in others, gives a person the incentive to develop and grow and also share life with humanity. The life-style "I'M OK—YOU'RE OK" is a prerequisite for a satisfying and a truly happy life. It can only be achieved by a deliberate effort to make it happen. The function of the

Adult within is to choose this philosophy of life and to insist that the Child and the Parent function within this environment.

No person or groups of persons have a corner on any one of these life positions. Representatives are to be found inside and outside religious institutions as well as in the secular world. Leaders and followers in every generation produce examples. Adolph Hitler, Albert Schweitzer, Mahatma Gandhi, Napoleon, Karl Marx, Tom Dooley, Marilyn Monroe, Martin Luther, Helen Keller, Martin Luther King, Jesus of Nazareth, John the Baptist, Paul, and Peter all had life positions and operated from them. Their biographies reflect their attitude toward self and others.

It matters greatly, for instance, how a clergyman sees himself and others. Examples of each of the above classifications can be easily found today within the religious establishment. The "I'M NOT OK—YOU'RE OK" clergyman may labor diligently in performing his ministry. He may be motivated to expend himself in helping others to find true happiness. He attends meetings, workshops, classes, seminars to improve his techniques of administration, preaching, counseling, and spiritual leadership. His unworthy image of himself encourages him to be a martyr in sacrifice and devotion. He studies, he tithes, he proselytes, he maintains a twenty-four-hour availability to his parishioners, he gives up on no one, he shares the problems of his people, he weeps with them, he does without, he carries his cross (the heavier the better), he constantly searches for ways of ministering to his people— because they deserve it. They are "OK." Even when they whine and complain and criticize and gossip and backslide and attack and manipulate and brag and hurt and cheat and sin. Even when they zero in their attacks on him. But the image of himself (and often the one he also forces on his family) continues "I'M NOT OK." In assuming the role of the "suffering servant" he delights that he can prove to himself, others, and even to God that unworthy as the clergyman is he is really trying; trying to beat hell, fighting the good fight, maintaining a feverish schedule, busier and more sacrificial than anyone else in the community, and he is proud of it. He is building up brownie points some place and he will eventually get his reward. He must prove himself, he must produce, he must strain and suffer. Because the image of himself is "I'M NOT OK" he glories in experiences that support this position. And he knows he is being observed and that no commitment or sacrifice or denial goes unrecorded in some bookkeeping system. He is "NOT OK" but he hopes that he will sometime earn the right to be "OK."

This is a good example of the Adapted Child who always does the right thing in order to receive strokes, accumulate stamps, and eventually trade the stamps in for some great prize.

This person may produce a great deal of good for the community. New churches and parish buildings are built, budgets raised, children educated, slums cleared, living conditions improved, hospitals constructed, prejudice attacked, injustices corrected, and other services performed. One basic truth he has ignored, however, is that God does not expect a man to be motivated from a "NOT OK" position. And all the victories against sin, graft, and inequality will not give him the satisfaction and joy he needs to be a whole and happy man. This clergyman misses the fact that his Master preached and lived and counseled from an "I'M OK—YOU'RE OK" position and insists that his first- and twentieth-century disciples do the same.

In the opinion of the writer the "I'M NOT OK—YOU'RE OK" position has soured many a clergyman's ministry especially in this generation of preachers. The choices available to this type of life-style are:

1. To continue to consider one's self as unworthy and by feverish activity to earn or deserve recognition. (Maintain the "I'M NOT OK—YOU'RE OK" position.)
2. Leave the ministry for secular work.
3. Escape to the security of a monastic order.
4. Turn to other escapes: alcohol, drug abuse, promiscuity.
5. Shift to the "I'M OK—YOU'RE NOT OK" position and desperately try to make up for all he has missed in life.
6. Shift to the "I'M NOT OK—YOU'RE NOT OK" position which leads to mental and/or physical suicide.
7. Or shift to the "I'M OK—YOU'RE OK" position which permits service to God and man, motivated by the Adult which limits the Parent and gives permission and supervision to the OK Natural Child within.

I suspect that the real motivation for many to seek a religious vocation begins out of a "I'M NOT OK" feeling. Even the calling of some of the leaders in biblical history began from this position. The book of Exodus tells of the calling of the great prophet Moses. At the time of his calling he was a shepherd working for his father-in-law Jethro. In the wilderness the call for service came and the response of

Moses shows he was in the "I'M NOT OK" attitude. The response to the call was in the following words:

"Who am I that I should go to Pharaoh, and bring the sons of Israel out of Egypt? (3:11)" "If I come to the people of Israel . . . what shall I say to them? (3:13)" "But behold, they will not believe me or listen to my voice, for they will say, 'The Lord did not appear to you. (4:1)' " Even after some miraculous proofs Moses even went on to say, "Oh, my Lord, I am not eloquent . . . I am slow of speech and of tongue (4:10)." "Oh, my Lord, send, I pray, some other person (4:13)."

The call of Isaiah also had dramatic "I'M NOT OK" overtones. "Woe is me! For I am lost; for I am a man of unclean lips (Isa. 6:5)." Both Moses and Isaiah accepted the challenge, changed their "I'M NOT OK" position to the more healthy one "I'M OK," and went out to serve God and man, and in the process found great satisfaction and joy.

If it is so important for a clergyman to evaluate his life-style and rationally choose the "I'M OK—YOU'RE OK" position it is also desirable that others do also. The housewife, the medical doctor, the teacher, the factory worker, the nurse, the farmer, the secretary, the sailor, the soldier, the marine, the airman, the student, the psychiatrist, the probation officer all can function more effectively from the "I'M OK—YOU'RE OK" position.

The housewife may seem to function effectively in the washing of dishes and the cleaning of floors from the "I'M NOT OK—YOU'RE OK" position. But her relationship with her children, her husband, her neighbors, her friends, could greatly benefit from the acceptance of and living the "I'M OK—YOU'RE OK" position. She (and every person) must evaluate her life-style, see herself as a worthwhile person who has control over her future, strengthen her confidence in her Adult and assume responsibility for her decisions.

One of the most difficult yet necessary tasks faced by a counselor is to help a person "like" herself/himself. A woman, for instance, who clings to the "I'M NOT OK—YOU'RE OK" position does not like herself. She probably has never liked herself. She does not want to like herself, for she believes that she is inadequate, inferior, not "OK." She keeps telling herself she is unattractive, untalented, awkward, stupid, lazy, too tall, too short, too loud, too quiet, etc. She doesn't like her hair color, her bustline, her eye color, her name, her voice, her hips, her legs, her teeth. She doesn't like the way she walks, sits, speaks, makes love, cooks, sews, or does housework. From early childhood she has not felt

"OK." Now that she is a grown person she still feels "NOT OK." Her Parent strongly reinforces this "NOT OK" feeling. Her Adult and Child are afraid of the Parent. Her Natural Child is afraid even to be exposed. Her Adapted Child cringes in the shadows. She seems to be an unhappy person who often seeks recognition (stroking) by a flurry of activity, much of which is wheel-spinning. Her Parent drives her Adapted Child to a dizzy round of bake sales, financial campaigns, clubs, church groups, chairmanships, political affiliations, lodges, cocktail parties, teas, coffees, receptions, as she associates with "OK" people. She must try to make up for her deficiencies. She feels she has to prove something to others—as though she, inferior as she is, has some right to keep on living. She feels she has to make up for all of her "inadequacies." Her Adapted Child tries to receive some recognition. But she really looks for reinforcement of the evidence that she is "NOT OK."

She has the same needs and the same choices as the "NOT OK" clergyman, especially the turning to alcohol, drugs, or promiscuity. Alcohol abuse and/or drug abuse gives her some temporary relief as the Parent can be temporarily anesthetized with a few drinks or a few pills. When she drinks or takes other medication to silence or muffle the demands of the Parent she is really in for trouble. The result of this is degrading and further reinforces her "I'M NOT OK" position. Alcohol or drug abuse first silences the Parent, then the Adult is affected leaving only the Child in control. This has a disastrous effect upon lives, marriages, homes, and relationships.

She may turn to sexual contacts outside her marriage just to obtain stroking. She is not, therefore, satisfied at home because the hunger for recognition, approval, and stroking is so strong and demanding she encourages the advances of men just to be noticed and touched. Frequently the contacts are strictly impersonal with no emotional investment being offered or expected.

The guilt produced by promiscuity also reinforces the "I'M NOT OK" feeling. The one who could sleep with anyone finds she cannot sleep with herself. She feels unworthy of her husband's love and the respect of her children. They are elevated to a higher level on the scale while she topples to new depths. More and more she feels, "I'M NOT OK—YOU'RE OK."

It is rare for a person who operates from an "I'M OK—YOU'RE OK" life-style to need the services of either the psychiatrist or the counselor. The ones who do come for assistance are to be found in the other three positions. The therapist can render valuable assistance by teaching the fundamentals of Transactional Analysis and encouraging the person to strengthen the Adult to evaluate the life's position, control the Parent, supervise the Child, rationally choose the "I'M OK— YOU'RE OK" position, and to operate from this approach. A new revelation can captivate the person when he realizes that he can change, he can be in control, and he is a worthwhile, responsible person.

It is amazing that individuals come in such assorted shapes, sizes, and personalities yet they can all be classified as being in one of the four life-styles. No two people are alike. Even their hands, their fingers, their fingerprints are unique. When we are shaped, the mold is shattered never to be used again. Even identical twins differ from one another. Having the same heredity and environment should produce sameness in personality and life positions but the rule is: there is no rule to follow. The first life position "I'M NOT OK—YOU'RE OK" is accepted on the basis of feeling. Later when the Adult is stronger, the Adult may accept this position without question or it may look for a more satisfying position.

Even more amazing than the uniqueness of persons is the fact that individuals can consciously change their life positions when the current one seems to thwart life and another offers more opportunities.

One of the attractions to the magnetic person of Jesus Christ is his life position of "I'M OK—YOU'RE OK." Persons of all ages and all professions recognize this quality. This has been the basis of friendship with him or opposition to his cause. He has the unique ability to accept persons, not for their *past* but for their *potential*. He sees all people as potential shareholders in the kingdom of God, being accepted not for what they pretend to be but for their capacity to live the principle of "I'M OK—YOU'RE OK." He can see through hypocrisy, prejudices, fears, hang-ups of the self-righteous as well as the calluses on the hands and tongues of fishermen, or the gaudy dress of the prostitutes. He fights prejudging, injustice, inequality, and hate by exposing his love to all and asking only love in return. Some men have rejected him and his love, but he sees no one as hopeless.

His "YOU'RE OK" position includes many who are living without hope. Females of the first century counted for little except as conveniences for men and producers of children. Outside the home they were without value. Even in the temple and synagog they were seated apart from the men and forced to observe rather than participate. To take an active part in social, economic, or political activities was beyond their highest hope. Jesus struck the first blow for women's liberation when he accepted them as "OK."

He also elevated the position of children. Those who were once tolerated now had great potential projected into them. The disciples sometimes "got up-tight" when little children were brought by mothers and fathers as they came to training sessions. But Jesus not only used them as examples of the right attitude for entrance into the kingdom of heaven; he also told the disciples and other grownups that they would never enter the kingdom until they learned the open and unsophisticated qualities of children.

Occupations such as tax collector, prostitute, professional serviceman, fisherman, which would seem to disqualify a person from entrance into discipleship, were looked at, not for the ugliness and pain they sometimes produced, but for the fact that they were pursued by people who had needs as well as potential. Jesus hated sin but loved the sinner. Most of all he hated the fact that persons tolerated the situation and ostracized those who provided the services. Who patronized the prostitutes, for instance? And who maintained the system that tolerated this evil?

3

Jesus Had a
Liberated Child

Jesus was not a great moralist, philosopher, or theologian by modern standards; for his approach to life, his fellowman, and God was simple and childlike. To be an authority in these scholarly fields is to have a complicated vocabulary, a grasp of every major school of thought, an analytical approach to each problem area, a prolific writing ability, plus the required academic credentials and position. Jesus had none of these.

Religion to Jesus was not the mastering of current systematic theology but his natural response to the love of God. To him the reality of God was as basic a fact as breathing and eating. Service to God and man was neither the giving of blind obedience to a legalistic code, however sacred or traditional, nor a concentrated studying of all that was written on these subjects. As a flower is drawn open by the warmth and light of the sun, exposing its beauty and releasing its fragrance, so Jesus responded to the love of God. This response was not the Adapted Child quivering under the authoritarian demands of the Parent, not just the logical approach of the Adult, but the approach of the Natural Child who brought the beautiful gifts of openness, wonder, responsiveness, spontaneity, self-abandon, anticipation, faith, imagination, love, sensuousness, humility, enthusiasm, creativity, optimism, unsophistication, and genuineness. These are the qualities of the "OK" Child and the prerequisites for entrance into the kingdom of heaven.

Jesus possessed these qualities. They did not lie dormant inside of him, afraid to respond to the love of God, but radiated through his entire personality. Jesus felt comfortable in exposing his Natural Child dimension to the world because he had an "I'M OK—YOU'RE OK" life-style. He looked at life, faced the facts and data that education, training, and experience had given him, and with this Adult dimension he made decisions and established goals. His Adult also dealt with the Parent dimension in him, the right and the wrong, the good and the bad, the correct and the incorrect, the legal and the illegal. This Parent dimension contained all the authoritarian inputs of Mary, Joseph, and rabbinical teaching, storing up this information until about the age of six. The traditional prejudices, favoritism, nationalism, eschatology of Judaism must also have been stored up in his Parent dimension as they were recorded by other young Jewish males of his day. It was as though Mary, Joseph, and Jewish tradition lived inside of him throughout his brief thirty-three years of life.

But the Adult of Jesus not only was busy giving a rational foundation for belief and truth but had two additional functions. Inputs from the Parent dimension had to be evaluated and sometimes silenced, and the Natural Child had to be encouraged and liberated. This was the truth that made him free.

Did the liberation of the Child take place in the home at Nazareth before or when the family made the historic trip to the holy city of Jerusalem when Jesus was twelve years of age? Did it take place after the baptism of Jesus, when there was an intense struggle within the person of Jesus between the Parent and the Adapted Child, with the Adult silencing both? Or did it happen sometime after the beginning of Jesus' ministry when Jesus shifted his outreach from a specialized ministry to "the lost sheep of the house of Israel" after his Adult had noted that only a limited number of Jews were responding to his invitation into the kingdom of God, and that the Gentiles seemed anxious and ready to respond to his love? Just when the Natural Child was liberated by the Adult of Jesus is unknown; but that the "OK" Child was an active and powerful force in his life has much supporting evidence.

The theme of the teaching, preaching, and life of Jesus was "the kingdom of heaven." Early in his ministry his approach carried the stern manner of John the Baptist as Jesus preached, "Repent and believe (Mark 1:15)," "Repent, for the kingdom of heaven is at hand (Matt. 4:17)." This is the approach of the Parent seeking a response in the

Adapted or "NOT OK" Child. Later he counseled, "Truly, I say to you, whoever does not receive the kingdom of God like a child shall not enter it (Mark 10:15)." This is the response of the Natural or "OK" Child, after the Adult has silenced the demands of the Parent and given permission for the Child to respond.

The method of illustrating the many facets of the kingdom of heaven was through parables or stories. These glimpses of the beauty of the kingdom of heaven, the significance of God's loving and eternal relationship with his family, came through the Natural Child of Jesus to the Natural Child of the people. The imagery appealed to and whetted the appetite and imagination of the Natural Child in both the teacher and the pupil. A farmer went forth to sow seed, a housewife baked bread, a fisherman cast his nets into the sea, a merchant searched for fine pearls, a king gave a marriage feast, a real estate man found a treasure in a field, a judge was hearing a case, a steward was asked to give an accounting, a woman lost a coin, a shepherd found a lost sheep, a father found a lost son; people were asked to consider lilies, sparrows, salt, oil lamps, new wine, water, yeast, money, mustard seed, goats, houses, fig trees, grape vines, and sand. The parables could be the basis of study by the Adult, using logic and analysis to make training allegories; but the real message was quite simple and had to be "understood" through the feelings of the Natural Child who alone possessed the key that unlocked the secrets of the kingdom of heaven (Matthew 13:10ff). This was the reason Jesus used parables; unless the hearer could liberate his Natural Child, he would hear the words but miss the meaning. Only those who could muster the Natural Child to hear the parables could enter the kingdom of heaven. He declared, "I thank thee, Father, Lord of heaven and earth, that thou has hidden these things from the wise and understanding and revealed them to babes; yea, Father, for such was thy gracious will (Matt. 11:25–26)."

The miracles similarly were signs that the kingdom of heaven was present and available to those who could respond through the Natural Child. Those who were Parent or Adult oriented often witnessed a marvelous event or mysterious happening but only those whose Natural Child was awakened could appreciate what was really involved.

It is suggested that the Natural Child of Jesus performed the many miracles recorded in the New Testament and that unless they were approached and observed by the Natural Child in others the fact that they were signs of the kingdom was missed. The Natural Child finds miracles not only believable but also desirable. A hard-headed "Let's look at the facts," "What has been done in the past?" and "What's your authority for doing this?" kept many from appreciating the signs of the kingdom in the first century and other centuries. But for those who possess the qualities of the Natural Child, the signs are beautiful illustrations of God with us. Jesus had a Natural Child that was open to the love of God and expected God to give signs and symbols of his power and care.

Jesus taught people the who, when, where, why, and how of prayer and revealed not only the faith behind his prayer life but also the mechanics of prayer. He began by saying, "Pray then like this: 'Our Father who art in heaven (Matt. 6:9).' " In the master prayer the imagery of reverence, the will of God, daily bread, forgiveness, temptation, deliverance are all in the terminology and imagery that the Natural Child understands and appreciates. This was not the prayer model of an Adapted Child trembling in fear before an unpredictable authority figure but of an open and responsive "OK" Child turning naturally to one he loves and trusts for both physical and spiritual sustenance. Jesus lived in both the physical and spiritual dimensions. What a beautiful model of the liberated Natural Child of Jesus that he openly shared with others!

The calling of the disciples was not Parent-Adapted Child: "Hey you, get over here and get over here quickly; I'm ordering you to report for work!" It was not a logical approach to a profession citing the income and fringe benefits of a specialized occupation (Adult-Adult). It was the Natural Child of Jesus to the Natural Child of those challenged with the words, "Follow me." One is reminded of the game, "Follow the Leader," which Jesus taught the disciples how to play. "I will make you fishers of men (Matt. 4:19)" appeals to the Natural Child. Its imagery and wonder can only be felt, not rationally understood. It is wondered what the rough fishermen ever said to their friends about the new job they went to after leaving their fishing boats and nets, and whether family and friends ever understood why grown men would ever respond to such a nebulous calling. But they did respond and the Natural Child knew why. The Adult and the Parent had only contempt for such foolishness.

Such were the critics of Jesus in his ministry. He was accused of keeping bad company (Matthew 9:11), of blasphemy (Matthew 26:65), of insanity (Mark 3:21), of being possessed with devils (John 7:20), of breaking the sabbath (John 9:16), and of treason (John 19:12). He was drawn to the outcasts, the sick, the suffering, the rejects of society, the sinners. But these people seemed to have a capability that the "normal" people lacked, and that was the ability to liberate their Child to respond to his love. These rejects of humanity seemed to have little trouble in silencing the Parent and giving permission to the Child. And great things happened to them and with them when the Natural Child of Jesus brought about a response in the Natural Child of the people. Jesus went to cocktail parties, dinners, discussion groups, wedding feasts; he associated with women, children, tax collectors, and prostitutes. For this the critics said, "Behold, a glutton and a drunkard, a friend of tax collectors and sinners (Matt. 11:19)!" Was it logic (Adult) that caused Jesus to identify with these persons? Was it a Parent-Adapted Child (NOT OK Child) relation (I'M OK—YOU'RE NOT OK)? Or was he one of them and they one with him, all having the qualities of the Natural Child in control?

The rejects of society, those without material resources or family name, the outcasts, the untouchables, those who appeared to be subnormal or atypical, those who either by a physical or emotional deformity felt outside the mainstream of living often gained great hope in living close to the personality and spirit of Jesus. They also had something to say to those who were content to ignore the cries of humans in need. Only a person who has known life from curbstone level can understand what it feels like to be a human reject.

Jesus seemed to have the ability to size up people and situations and see right through pretense and sham. This ability is also enjoyed by some sensitive children who are unimpressed with fakery, hypocrisy, or self-righteousness. It is the insight of the Natural Child. It is also the quality that sees worth in humble places and poverty in high places. Jesus in the dimension of the Natural Child had these insights and those with similar motivations were attracted to him. Children were drawn to him. They loved to be with him. They responded to his love. They felt comfortable in his presence and he shared their enthusiasm. "Do not hinder them," Jesus said to the grownups; "Become like them," was his counsel. His guidance was, "Liberate your Child." Persons of all ages who were able to respond to his love were able to accomplish this feat and enjoy his love and share his friendship.

Friendship was the favorite description used by Jesus for this unique relationship:

> This is my commandment, that you love one another as I have loved you. Greater love has no man than this, that a man lay down his life

for his friends. You are my friends if you do what I command you. No longer do I call you servants, . . . I have called you friends, for all that I have heard from my Father I have made known to you. You did not choose me, but I chose you and appointed you that you should go and bear fruit and that your fruit should abide.

—John 15:12–16

Jesus asked people of all chronological ages to be his friends, to share life with him. Friendships can be sought for a variety of reasons, some of which can be selfish, where persons are used, abused, taken advantage of, exploited. The friendship of Jesus was from an "I'M OK—YOU'RE OK" life-style. The religious leaders of the first century pictured their followers as inadequate and undeveloped, "NOT OK." It was a Parent-Adapted Child relationship. At times it appears that there were overtones of this in the relationships of Jesus, especially with his disciples. One time he told them, "No longer do I call you servants (slaves)." Many people seem to need an authority figure and want a leader to whom they can give obedience. But the only obedience Jesus requested was to love, and this is the motivation of the Natural Child.

When Jesus faced the cross it was not the Adapted Child giving blind obedience to a demanding Parent, although a struggle of this nature took place within him in the Garden of Gethsemane just prior to the events of the crucifixion. He prayed so earnestly that "his sweat became like great drops of blood falling down upon the ground (Luke 22:44)." The Adult finally took control, made a decision, silenced the Parent and again released the "OK" Child, who was then free to "lay down his life for his friends," as he had counseled his friends to do earlier. Jesus did not have a martyr complex. He was not self-destructive. He loved life. But he had to deal with the same temptations and struggles that other humans face. "For we have not a high priest who is unable to sympathize with our weaknesses, but one who in every respect has been tempted as we are, yet without sinning (Heb. 4:15)."

Many temptations are a conflict within a person between the Adapted Child and Parent dimension. The Adapted Child wants, lusts, whines, demands, complains, and has an unending list of what he justly deserves. If there is such a thing as evil personified in a devil or Satan, he would probably approach a person in the dimension of Adapted Child who does not feel "OK." Victory over temptation comes, not by trying to appease the demands of the Adapted Child, but by the Adult taking control of the Parent who establishes boundaries for the Adapted Child, so the "OK" Child can again feel free to enjoy the goodness of life.

Jesus had a liberated Child. This was possible because his Adult was in control to evaluate life, look at the facts, make decisions, set goals, but also restrict the Parent when the Parental inputs were not helpful. The Adult also said to the Natural Child, "It's OK to enjoy life and be at peace." Jesus generally had an "I'm OK—You're OK" outlook on life. The few exceptions will be discussed in the later chapter which deals with "the Parent in Jesus." When Parental injunctions restricted growth, then these were evaluated and eventually replaced with rational motivations. In this environment the Natural Child was encouraged to come to the surface and enjoy life.

Only a person who is at peace with God, his fellowman, and himself can take the chance of exposing the Natural Child. Jesus had this ability. When this process began and who was responsible for it can only be surmised. Evidently Jesus grew up in a home where it was comfortable to expose the Natural Child. It is believed that within the loving atmosphere of that humble home in Nazareth, Joseph and Mary not only provided the basics of physical, mental, and religious growth but also encouraged Jesus and his siblings to enjoy the goodness of life. It is believed that both Mary and Joseph had an "I'm OK—You're OK" life-style and knew how and when to liberate the Natural Child. The first we ever hear of Mary and Joseph shows their ability to come through in the dimension of the Natural Child. Both were visited by an angel, and only persons who can muster the Natural Child have the perception to communicate with angels (Luke 1:26ff, Matthew 1:18ff). A young virgin received the love of God in her body in a special way. She was enthusiastic and filled with wonder that God had chosen her to be the mother of Jesus. It was not the Adapted Child in blind obedience. It was the "OK" Child who responded to the love of God. Joseph also responded to the love of God and took his virgin, though pregnant, to be his wife. He received the counsel of God with his "OK" Child. He was unconcerned about whether there were scientific facts to justify marriage to a pregnant virgin.

The ability of Jesus to be comfortable at a banquet or party, to be unthreatened by accusations of being a drunkard, a glutton, and irreligious, to be able to associate with the untouchables and undesirables, to tell beautiful stories illustrating the kingdom of heaven, to relate to persons outside Judaism, to worship and enjoy one's faith, to accept and expect miracles of faith—all these show that his early training in the home must have been a beautiful example of love in action. He seems to be generally free from political, national, and racial prejudice, strict denominational guidelines, a legalistic approach to ethical living, a ritualistic conception of religion and worship. He talked about dispensing truth that literally makes people free; free from the prejudices and hang-ups of men, free to enjoy the goodness of life, free to be optimistic about God and man, free to liberate the Child. This freedom which he talked about and lived probably had its basis and encouragement in the home.

Where, for instance, did he learn about leaven, lost coins, lost sheep, plowing and planting, fishing, flowers, birds, dogs, puppies, bread, wine, gardening, weeds, and friendship? Who taught him about dancing, games, singing, story telling, worship, loyalty, family living, family name, neighborliness, and love? Joseph, Mary, brothers, sisters, playmates, community had an effect upon his life and helped shape his personality.

He probably had an "OK" Child because he had "OK" Child experiences. He learned the lessons of trust, love, openness, wonder, and expectancy not only by observing his mother, father, and contemporaries but by exposing his Natural Child. The only boyhood experience of Jesus is recorded in Luke 2 where the small family journeyed to Jerusalem with relatives and friends to celebrate the feast of the Passover. Even at the age of twelve years Jesus was accepted as an "OK" person when he was on his own during this visit to the holy city. Mary and Joseph were shocked to find that on the return trip Jesus was not in the caravan. Returning to Jerusalem and searching for three days they found him in the temple, with the teachers. People were amazed at "his understanding and answers." His grasp of Judaism and its application to everyday living was of great interest to those who heard him. His openness to the truth with its vast practical value had a ring to it far different from memorized questions and answers of the traditionalists. His simple theology pictured God as a loving and caring heavenly Father; heaven was accessible to believers; all persons possessed the potential for being included in the family of God. Such perception in a young boy was indeed a compliment to the quality of life experienced in his home. His ability to clear away the dross and unessentials of custom and religion to expose the necessity of loving relationships was probably seen at this early age. His subsequent painful struggle with legalistic religion is developed in the section, "The Dimension in Jesus Called Parent."

He felt comfortable even in the temple environment, stating that this was truly, "My Father's house"—the way a person, also in the dimension of the Natural Child, would point out as he passed his home church, "That's my church." He was a little surprised that Mary and Joseph were upset at his side trip. Even at this early age he seemed to include others as family members—much to the surprise of his parents.

The amazement of the temple teachers concerning this twelve-year-old was not that he had an elaborate and complicated theology with all the right "God-words" and phrases, but that in a simple and practical way he expressed great insight into the nature and will of God. Using unsophisticated illustrations and stories, as well as early experiences with nature, people, family, and God, Jesus was able to share these insights with others. Religion was daily living and daily living was religion. Worship was as natural as breathing and eating. Serving God was not escaping from the world but enjoying the world with its goodness and love which God wanted to share with man. The life of Jesus, even at the age of twelve years, was the personalizing of the doxology, "Praise God from whom all blessings flow." It was his Natural Child. When he grew to manhood he rarely lost this approach to life. For this was the quality of life he talked about and lived and offered to share with his contemporaries of every age. Since that time there have been great scholars, knowledgeable teachers, disciplined martyrs, able philosophers, sensitive humanitarians, prophets, priests, and kings. Perhaps their expertise and their competence exceeded that of the Nazarene. But the ability to live, love, enjoy life, and be an effective member of God's family on earth has never been better personified than in the son of a poor carpenter in Galilee, for Jesus gave of himself and drank deeply from the well of life in the dimension of the Natural Child.

For Jesus, devotion to God and service to fellowman was not motivated by fear, blind obedience, legalism, guilt, or inadequacy ("NOT OK" Child). The Adapted or "Not OK" Child feverishly tries to earn peace of mind by getting the Parent off his back. He looks for ways of earning brownie stamps so he can see his spiritual progress and thus be assured that he is getting closer to heaven. But he resists the idea of getting to heaven as long as he can so he can be sure to have assembled sufficient brownie stamps to earn his reward.

A Buddhist once said to the author, "You Christians are always talking about the beauty and joy in heaven. Why do you resist so much the fact of death and try to postpone it as long as possible?" Many people would answer, "To save more brownie stamps," but probably the answer of Jesus would be that heaven is not "pie in the sky, by and by," but accessible now, to be enjoyed here as well as in the hereafter. The projection of sitting on a cloud for eternity, strumming a harp, turns many people off, and rightly so. But the idea of a loving relationship with others and God that can be experienced now and will continue forever is worth having. And Jesus and you and I enter this relationship through the Natural Child.

Faith in God and man is through the Natural Child. The awareness and enjoyment of the environment is through the Natural Child. Love is the motivation of the Natural Child. Like the broad jumper who runs in a straight line and at a certain point makes a leap in the same direction, so the Adult dimension in man gives direction and satisfaction to our lives. But there comes a time when the Adult must take the leap of faith. When this happens the Natural Child is liberated, and at the same time it needs to be supervised by reason and logic. The Natural Child is not inhibited by the Adult but is encouraged by it. Discipleship of Jesus is not by order or logic, but is the Natural Child responding to a loving relationship.

When Jesus called the fishermen to be his disciples he did not direct them or logically tell them about all the small print in the contract but said, "Follow me, and I will make you fishers of men (Matt. 4:19)." To Matthew, the tax collector, he said, "Follow me (Mark 2:14)," to Philip he said, "Follow me (John 1:43)." He later stated to the disciples, "You did not choose me, but I chose you and appointed you that you should go and bear fruit and that your fruit should abide (John 15:16)." He made it clear that the material rewards would be small, the sacrifices many, the cross-bearing heavy, the spiritual satisfaction great, the joy of service without measure or termination. He said, "These things I have spoken to you, that my joy may be in you, and that your joy may be full (John 15:11)." "I came that they may have life, and have it abundantly (John 10:10)."

He did not order them (Parent-Adapted Child). He did not make them feel obligated or inferior (Parent-Adapted Child). He did not logically draw up a union contract, citing benefits and fringe benefits (Adult-Adult). He only said, "Follow me" (Natural Child-Natural Child). The power of his personality was inviting, his "OK"-ness was contagious, his friendship, love and faith in God were captivating and genuine, his openness and simplicity helped to make life meaningful, and the disciples responded. As in a childlike game of "Follow the Leader," the twelve men of the first century took a chance with him. He only promised to be with them; he never asked them to go anywhere alone. What he had to offer them was a pearl of great value, worth the investment of their most important and valuable asset, their personalities. It was not until after his crucifixion and resurrection that they really "understood" with their hearts. The proof of their dedication and discipleship is that they literally turned the world upside down for their risen Lord, not only after he promised to be with them in spirit, but when they experienced this fact, for the Holy Spirit is the extension of the Natural Child of Jesus and spoke to the need and invitation of the disciples' Natural Child.

The Natural Child of Jesus is visible throughout the Gospel account. It is not accidental that his reputation was tarnished by those who could not "Liberate their Child." Those who were Parent- or Adult-oriented accused him of violations of good order and decency. A person gains a reputation by where he goes, what he does, and with whom he relates. Those who were bound by the rigidity of legalism and formalism could not experience the warmness of Jesus' love (Natural Child).

The Gospel of John (chapter 2) records an historic miracle happening at Cana in Galilee where Jesus, Mary, and the disciples were present. It is true for the twentieth century and also true for the first century that when you give a party, have a wedding reception or some other social event, you want your guests to come in the dimension of the Natural Child, supervised by the Adult. The frowning displeasure of the Parent or the shoptalk of the Adult are not welcome or appropriate at social gatherings. This was true for Jesus, Mary, and the disciples at that first-century wedding reception for at this early time festivities might last over a period of a week. The supply of wine gave out and Mary became concerned about the embarrassment of the host. There are many unanswerable questions surrounding this incident, but some facts remain: It was a time of happiness and celebration; Jesus and his disciples were involved; the wine supply failed; Jesus performed the miracle; his glory was manifested, and the disciples had their faith strengthened. Miracles of faith happened in the first century and they happen in this and other centuries. The necessary ingredient seems to be the liberation of the Natural Child for the witnesses as well as the miracle worker. Without this atmosphere the ability to perform miracles seems to be seriously limited. The necessary ingredients for miracles are: expectancy, faith, trust, wonder, openness, creativity, imagination, hope, responsiveness, anticipation, self-acceptance; and these are the qualities of the Natural Child, liberated and supervised by the Adult. It is permissible and desirable that the Natural Child be released and encouraged. The Parental hang-ups and criticism must be silenced; the Adult must furnish data and facts where these are available; but it is only when the Adult has given permission to the Natural Child that a miracle can be produced as well as experienced.

To demand proof of a miracle is to miss the miracle. To insist upon scientific examination or rational explanation will cause the miracle to disintegrate like a mist before the rising sun. To ask for a miracle or sign in order to trust a person, believe him, or follow his teaching would be unproductive. Magic and sleight-of-hand tricks can be rationally understood and duplicated. But a miracle is a "sign" that the kingdom of heaven is accessible and can only be appreciated and experienced by the person whose Natural Child has been liberated by the Adult.

There are many miracles recorded in the New Testament performed by the Natural Child dimension of Jesus and later by the disciples. That they were not performed haphazardly shows the Adult was supervising the Natural Child. There are healing miracles upon the bodies and minds of people. There are miracles that take place in nature, stilling the storm (Matthew 8:26), walking on the sea (Matthew 14:25), feeding the multitude (Matthew 14:15), draught of fish (Luke 5:6, John 21:6), tribute money (Matthew 17:24); the dead are raised (Luke 7:11ff, John 11:1ff), the blind see (Matthew 9:27), the deaf hear (Mark 7:33), the lame walk (Acts 3:7)—all show the variety of New Testament miracles. Two qualities seem to be necessary: (1) The liberation of the Natural Child in the person performing the miracle, and (2) the liberation of the Natural Child in those witnessing and learning from the "sign."

There were times when Jesus and the disciples were unable to perform the "signs" of the kingdom due to a sterile or unfriendly atmosphere of the people. In his hometown of Nazareth it is spoken, "And they took offence at him. But Jesus said to them, 'A prophet is not without honor except in his own country and in his own house.' And he did not do many mighty works there, because of the unbelief (Matt. 13:57–58)."

When he went to a town where a little girl had died and the father had asked for the presence of the Master, coming into the house the first thing he did was to dismiss the pagan professional mourners, flute players, and crowd. Then alone with those who had brought the necessary ingredient called faith, which is the motivation of the Natural Child, Jesus raised up the child (Matthew 9:18ff).

Perhaps Jesus' diagnoses of the first-century afflictions would not meet modern standards of scientific objectivity ("he has a demon," "a demon possesses her," "an issue of blood," "a demoniac," etc.). His techniques would probably be frowned upon as primitive and unsanitary (using spit, clay, water). Still, miracles were accomplished in the first century. People motivated by faith have seen these as signs that the kingdom of heaven is in our midst, and much good has come of their inclusion in the Gospels.

When John the Baptist was in prison and sent word to Jesus by messenger, inquiring whether Jesus were really the Messiah, the one who was to usher in the kingdom of heaven, Jesus sent back the reply: "Go and tell John what you hear and see: the blind receive their sight and the lame walk, lepers are cleansed and the deaf hear, and the dead are raised up, and the poor have good news preached to them. And blessed is he who takes no offense at me (Matt. 11:4-6)."

The feeding of the five thousand persons recorded in John 6 seems to contradict the assumption that a miracle could happen only in an atmosphere of faith, since the crowd who witnessed the miracle completely missed the meaning of it. They recognized Jesus as a wonder worker and having some admirable qualities that a political leader could exploit, that of multiplying a nation's food supply.

The experience happened near the Sea of Galilee. A crowd of people had witnessed the healing ministry of Jesus. They followed him as he attempted to find some rest and peace. In a lonely and hilly area Jesus once again taught the people. It was the time of Passover, an annual observance of the deliverance of the Israelites from the hands of the Egyptians. Toward the end of the day when everyone was tired and hungry, Jesus said to Philip, "How are we to buy bread, so that these people may eat?" There was neither the money nor the resources there to feed the people. At this time Andrew's Natural Child said enthusiastically, "There is a lad here with the family picnic basket containing five loaves and two small fish." Then his Adult cautioned him, "But what are they among so many?"

It was Jesus who responded by saying, "Tell the people to sit down on the grass and relax. Let us with faith lift our needs to God." Be aware of the fact that before this he had taught the disciples to pray, "Give us this day our daily bread." Everyone present must have known that God had fed the Children (Note the word children) of Israel with bread for forty years while they were in a wilderness. History was about to repeat itself. The time was ripe for a sign of the kingdom.

The attention was focused upon a little boy who had custody of the family's meal. When the cry had gone out to see what resources were available this little boy responded, "Here, Jesus, you can have our picnic supper." The spontaneous response of the boy to the cry of human need has earned for him the acclaim of the centuries. We do not know his name or what happened to him later. But we do know that he had a Natural Child dimension and that miracles happen when people are motivated in this dimension.

The prayer of Jesus in giving thanks to God seemed to produce the required atmosphere for the miracle to become a reality. Evidently there were some who were able to muster the Natural Child. Five thousand people were fed, twelve baskets of leftovers were gathered up after the dinner, and the people responded, "This is indeed the prophet who is to come into the world." But the miracle was tarnished when the people plotted how they could take Jesus by force to make him their king. This incident gave Jesus an opportunity later to make spiritual application that he was the "bread of life," which also is a dimension of life to be understood and accepted, not by the Parent or the Adult, but by the Natural Child.

Notice some of the expressions that have been used to describe Jesus:

"Alpha and Omega," "Author and Finisher of our faith," "Beloved Son," "Branch," "Captain of Salvation," "Chief Shepherd," "Deliverer," "Door," "Good Shepherd," "Head of the Church," "Holy One of Israel," "Horn of Salvation," "Image of God," "King of kings," "Lamb of God," "Life," "Light of the World," "Lord of lords," "Man of Sorrows," "Mediator," "Messiah," "Morning Star," "Nazarene," "Only Begotten Son," "Prince of Peace," "Redeemer," "Resurrection and Life," "Rock," "Root of David," "Savior," "Shepherd and Bishop of Souls," "Son of David," "Son of God," "Son of man," "True Light," "True Vine," "Truth," "Word of God," and many others. These names of Jesus can become God-words directed by the Parent to prove religious orthodoxy. They can be written in creeds and recited over and over. They can be studied by the Adult and meaning can be read out of them and into them. But true understanding can come only through the Natural Child who appreciates vivid imagery, loud sounds, and exciting talk. These expressions can set the wheels of the Natural Child's imagination spinning and generating new thoughts and ideas. For this reason certain books of the Bible appeal to the curiosity and wonder of the Natural Child (viz. Revelation and Daniel). Other books like the

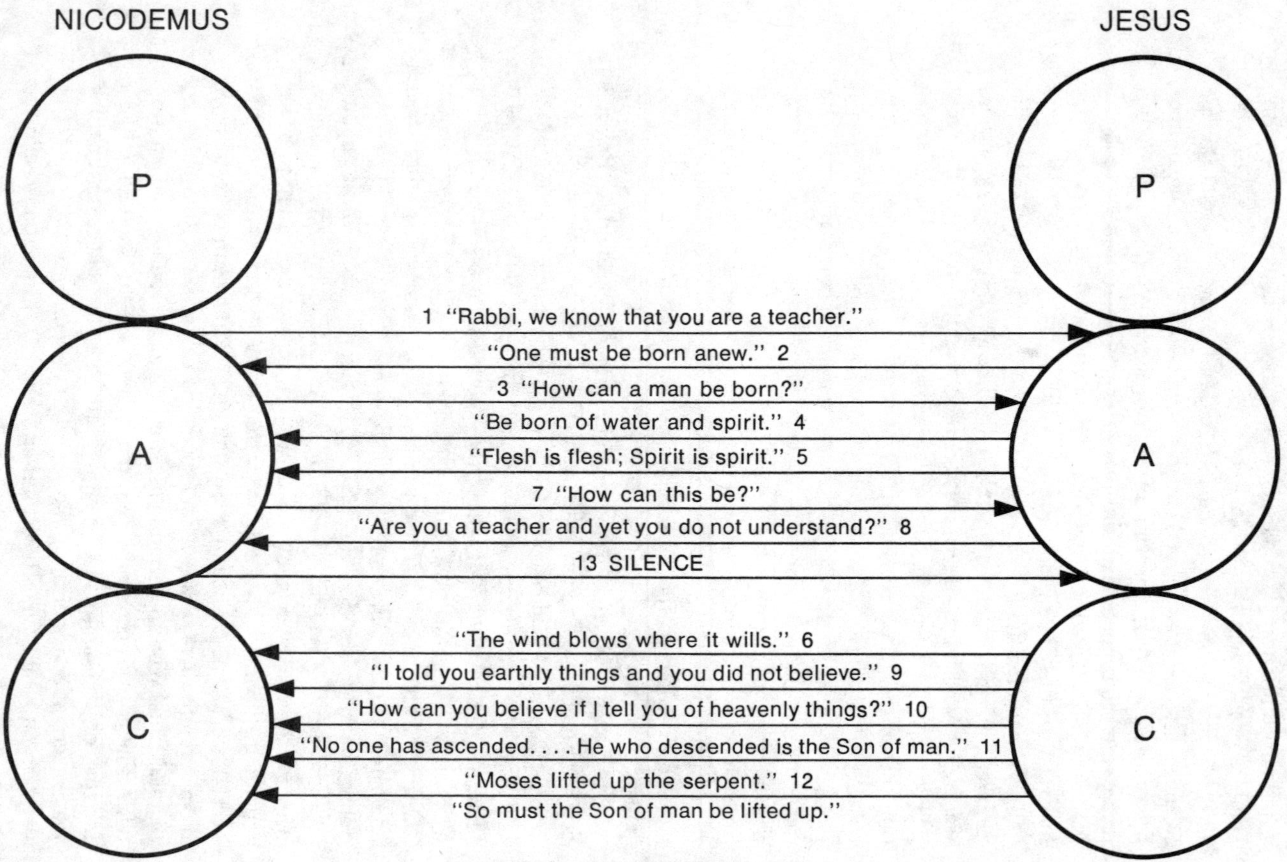

JESUS AND NICODEMUS
FIGURE 3

—JOHN 3:1-15

NICODEMUS

P

A

C

JESUS

P

A

C

1 "Rabbi, we know that you are a teacher."

"One must be born anew." 2

3 "How can a man be born?"

"Be born of water and spirit." 4

"Flesh is flesh; Spirit is spirit." 5

7 "How can this be?"

"Are you a teacher and yet you do not understand?" 8

13 SILENCE

"The wind blows where it wills." 6

"I told you earthly things and you did not believe." 9

"How can you believe if I tell you of heavenly things?" 10

"No one has ascended. . . . He who descended is the Son of man." 11

"Moses lifted up the serpent." 12

"So must the Son of man be lifted up."

Gospel of John should be read on one's knees by the Natural Child supervised by the Adult.

The dialogue that took place between Jesus and Nicodemus (John 3) illustrates not only the motivation of Jesus in the dimension of the Natural Child, but also the fact that some who were attracted to his personality found it very difficult to liberate this dimension within themselves and discover what the kingdom of heaven was all about (Figure 3). Nicodemus was an educated and respected man. He knew both the sacred and secular law. He was a good citizen, a member of the high Jewish court, a member of the Pharisee Party which gave strict adherence to minute details in following the teaching of the Hebrew religion. He was attracted to Jesus and secretly had an audience with him one night. He recognized that Jesus was a prophet, a miracle worker, sent from God. Though he was captivated by his message, he was quite unable to understand and apply his teaching. Knowledge of the law and the ability to use reason had always thrown light on teachers and theology before, but now these aids left Nicodemus bewildered and uncertain.

There was talk about reawakening the Natural Child as the key to understanding and living. Jesus said, "Unless one is born anew, he cannot see the kingdom of God." This point was met with the question, "How can a man be born when he is old? Can he enter a second time into his mother's womb and be born?" Though it may seem to be oversimplifying the teaching of Jesus, basically what Jesus was saying to Nicodemus was, "Liberate your (Natural) Child." To put this in other words would be, "Don't get hung up on legalism (Parent) nor upon reason (Adult). Both of these disciplines are helpful, but never at the expense of the Natural Child. Be content to give permission to your Natural Child, even if you have to silence the Parent. Recognize that entrance into the kingdom of God is not gained through your own ability, effort, or understanding. It must be accepted as a gift."

The Natural Child gleefully is ready to accept a gift, especially a gift that will be used and treasured. Entrance into the kingdom of God is the greatest and most sensuous gift available to mankind, for this gift can be experienced and enjoyed in this life and in the life to come. All the God-given senses can be used to experience it.

The kingdom of God was the central theme of Jesus. His teaching, his illustrations, his parables, his miracles, his signs, his sacraments, his church were all evidences of this important theme. Every place he went he talked of the kingdom of God. Everything he did was related to the coming of the kingdom of God. As he witnessed to large groups or on a one-to-one situation, this is what he talked about. He taught people to look for the kingdom of God, to work for its coming, to expect its coming, to be ready for its coming, to be willing to sacrifice for its coming, but mainly to be willing to accept its coming as important, necessary, and fulfilling.

The Natural Child possesses the necessary prerequisites for seeing the kingdom of God. The Natural Child lives in the unseen as well as the seen world. He understands the flesh and the spirit. He knows the reality of the wind, what it feels like, what it looks like when objects come under its control. Whether it is a sailboat being pushed along, tree branches waving at the clouds, or a kite responding to its pull, when the Natural Child is in control even something as commonplace as the wind is of great importance and wonder. The wind is reality. The wind is truth. Hence the Spirit is reality. The Spirit is truth.

Nicodemus was confused because he was unable at the time to muster his Natural Child and so he asked, "How can this be?" The answer of Jesus must have been given with a twinkle in his eye, "Are you a teacher of Israel, and yet you do not understand this?" The secrets and benefits of the kingdom of God are not to be obtained through logic or legalism. These tools are helpful in building an ethical system, setting realistic goals, and maintaining discipline. But they cannot dispense the kingdom of God nor counterfeit the feelings of the kingdom which are true happiness and joy.

The Gospel of John records another meaningful confrontation of Jesus with a person, this time a woman of Samaria who had come to the well at Sychar to draw water (John 4:5–42). Jesus was tired and thirsty. He stopped in the center of the city to rest at Jacob's well. The disciples went in search of food and Jesus remained at the well. A Samaritan woman came to fill her water jar. With his "OK" Child in control Jesus asked her for a drink (Figure 4). He had nothing to lower into the well to get water. He used a method that some modern authors have rediscovered: that to make a friend, rather than doing a favor for him, you ask him to do you a favor. This was unusual, for this person was a woman, a Samaritan woman, a divorcee, an adulteress, and a Gentile. These features would cause a faithful Jew to avoid the situation as though the person had a deadly, contagious disease.

Obviously the woman had some faith (Natural Child), but she kept the Adult in complete control. She had learned to be suspicious of foreigners, especially Jewish foreigners. She asked the question, " 'How

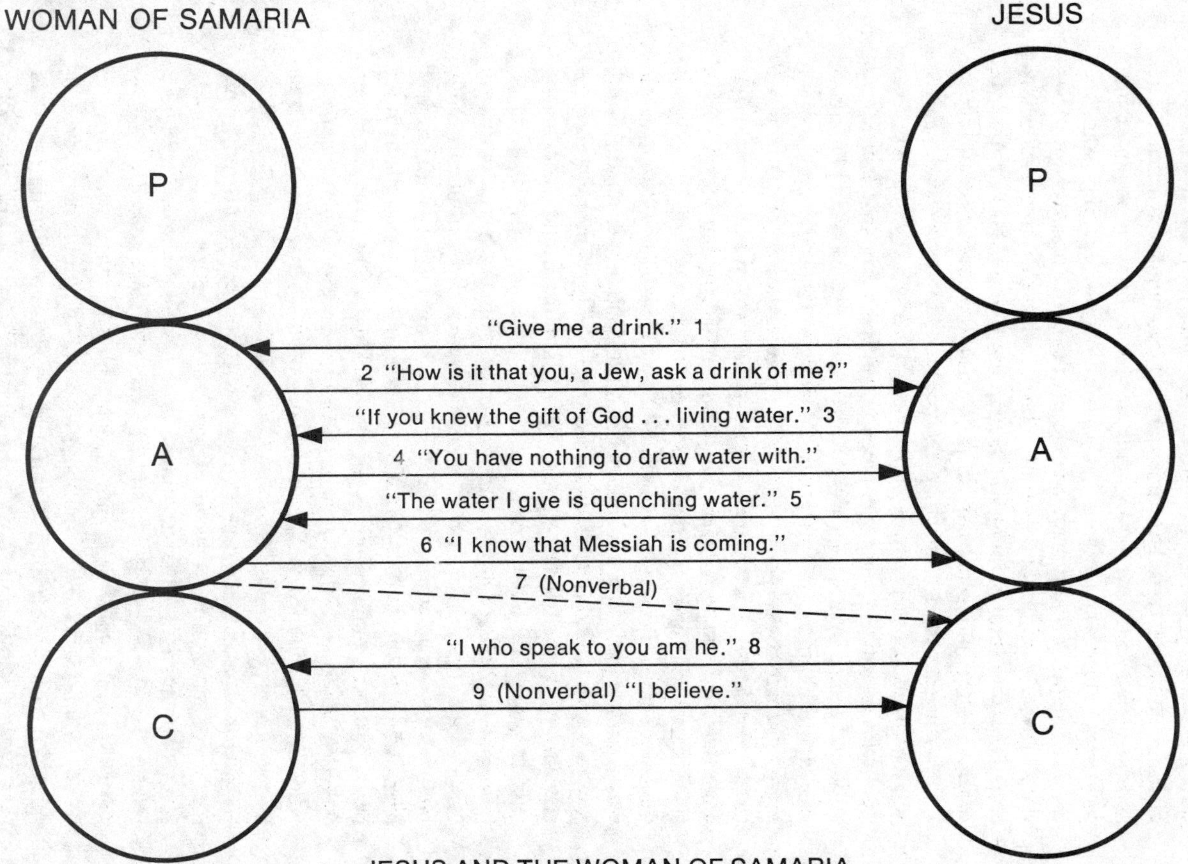

WOMAN OF SAMARIA

JESUS

P

A

C

P

A

C

"Give me a drink." 1

2 "How is it that you, a Jew, ask a drink of me?"

"If you knew the gift of God . . . living water." 3

4 "You have nothing to draw water with."

"The water I give is quenching water." 5

6 "I know that Messiah is coming."

7 (Nonverbal)

"I who speak to you am he." 8

9 (Nonverbal) "I believe."

JESUS AND THE WOMAN OF SAMARIA
FIGURE 4

—JOHN 4:5-42

is it that you, a Jew, ask a drink of me, a woman of Samaria?' For Jews have no dealings with Samaritans." The answer of Jesus reached for a response in her "OK" Child, "If you knew the gift of God, and who it is that is saying to you, 'Give me a drink,' you would have asked him, and he would have given you living water." The woman missed the point. She was able to see only that Jesus was hardly able to give anyone water when he obviously had no equipment to lower into the well. Jesus was talking about the "fountain of youth" and the woman could think only about the water fountain in the center of town. With her Adult in control she was interested only in facts; hard, proven facts.

Again Jesus tried to reach her Natural Child when he said, "Every one who drinks of this water will thirst again, but whoever drinks of the water that I shall give him will never thirst; the water that I shall give him will become in him a spring of water welling up to eternal life." She missed the point again. Thinking only of the facts and the labor of carrying water she responded, "Sir, give me this water, that I may not thirst, nor come here to draw." The Adult was still the motivating dimension. It is suspected that this person must have felt "NOT OK" (like others who have felt the pain of prejudice over a long period of time and can easily develop a "NOT OK" Child) especially when she was in the presence of a Jew. There was little doubt in her mind that the Jewish people were "God's Chosen People." She lived in an atmosphere of feeling "NOT OK," for she, her family, and her friends were on the outside looking in, but never being able to come in. They believed in God, but in the eyes of those in the "in group," the Samaritans were considered to be an inferior race of people. The really painful part of the prejudging is that after a while the person on the receiving end of prejudice begins feeling "NOT OK." To combat prejudice, logic must be used, facts examined, decisions made. This is the function of the Adult. The Adult of the Samaritan woman was strong and in control. The Natural Child was hiding in a corner, afraid of making its presence known.

In the discussion that followed some beautiful statements came from the lips of Jesus on the subjects of worship and the nature of God. He said, "The hour is coming, and now is, when the true worshipers [Natural Child supervised by the Adult] will worship the Father in spirit [Natural Child] and truth [Adult], for such the Father seeks to worship him. God is spirit, and those who worship him must worship in spirit and truth." Then the woman began to understand and to speak of the Messiah who was to come. She opened her heart and exposed some of the personal views and hopes she had. She exposed her ability to take a chance and share her feelings. She believed that the coming of the Messiah was to usher in the kingdom of God, where all men would be recognized as brothers, where pain, prejudice, and spiritual ignorance would be conquered. She showed that she possessed the dimension of life that was filled with hope, wonder, enthusiasm, expectancy, and faith which are the qualities of the Natural Child.

Jesus said, "I who speak to you am he." He told her a secret, and the woman left in such a hurry that she forgot to take her water jar with her. Quickly she returned to her home and with her voice quivering with excitement she told her friends about the experience. To show the quality of her witness to her friends, Jesus and the disciples stayed two additional days in the Gentile city. These Gentiles responded to the Natural Child of Jesus. They rejoiced in his "Good News." He was pleased to discover that these Gentiles were willing to activate the Natural Child and to receive and share his love and compassion, a quality that few of his countrymen possessed.

That which attracted people to Jesus was not his logic, nor his scholarly pronouncements, but his love. Some persons responded to his love, others rejected him because he refused to conform to their stereotypes. The people were looking for Messiah to come. But Jesus did not profess the party line that they required. Most of the people wanted an authority figure who would make things right in the world. They wanted a leader who would once again make Jerusalem a major capital, a mighty power, a symbol of wealth. But Jesus saw his mission to be that of sharing the kingdom of heaven with men.

The transfiguration of Jesus, recorded in Matthew 17:1ff, shows Jesus and his disciples in the dimension of the Natural Child. Jesus took Peter, James, and John up a high mountain and there they had a great spiritual experience. Not only was there similarity to Moses' experience on the mountain, when it was necessary to veil his face (Exodus 34:33), but Jesus also had a radiance about him, and the disciples witnessed the experience. Moses and Elijah were "seen" to be talking with Jesus. Peter got so excited that he wanted to set up booths to honor the occasion, one for Moses, one for Elijah, and one for Jesus. Then there was a voice from heaven that said, "This is my beloved Son, with whom I am well pleased; listen to him (Matt. 17:5)." The disciples fell on their faces with fear, and wonder, and awe. But Jesus came and touched them and said, "Rise, and have no fear." When they opened their eyes, they saw only Jesus. This experience made a great impression on these disciples. They never forgot it.

Only people who have the Natural Child in control can see visions of Elijah and Moses, and hear a voice that says, "This is my beloved Son; listen to him." The response cannot come from the Adult who looks only at data and facts. It cannot be made by the Parent stating, "You will believe this or that. This is doctrine. You must accept it." The response does not come from the Adapted Child who fearfully anticipates a visitation of God. The response is awakened in the "OK Child" of Jesus and the disciples in the presence of God and God's servants, and cannot be logically explained, proven, or understood. But the Natural Child knows its truth.

The Natural Child of Jesus was seen in the way he lived, in the content of his teaching and preaching, and also in his ability to tell stories about the kingdom of God which are called parables. To understand his message, logic or the Adult can be of some benefit. But the real understanding of the parables and other symbols that he used can be grasped only through the feelings of the Natural Child. When people, including the disciples, had to ask what a parable meant, the true message was lost, for real understanding of the parables was through the "feelings" of the Natural Child. Love can be rationally discussed, its desirability explained, its beauty described, but really to be understood it has to be experienced through the Natural Child. Only when you are caught up in love, only when you love can you understand the meaning of love. The kingdom of heaven is the kingdom of love. You can talk about it, motivate people to seek it; but it is only when you respond to the love of God that you can know it, and it is with the Natural Child that you receive it. A preacher or teacher cannot dispense the kingdom of heaven. He can only describe its value and beauty, thus whet the appetite of the Natural Child. We cannot really build the kingdom of God; we can only accept and enjoy it.

There are over three dozen parables recorded in the Gospels. A variety of symbols are used to illustrate the many facets of the kingdom of heaven. Some of the parables are one-liners. Others are quite lengthy and involved. Several parables will be discussed below in order to show that the secret of the one telling the parable and the one who "understands," is through the dimension of the Natural Child (Figure 5).

> He also told this parable to some who trusted in themselves that they were righteous and despised others: "Two men went up into the

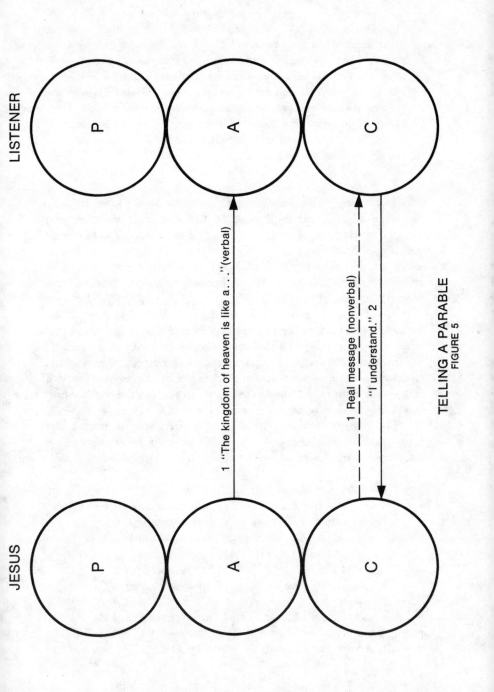

LISTENER

JESUS

P

A

C

P

A

C

1 "The kingdom of heaven is like a . . ." (verbal)

1 Real message (nonverbal)

"I understand." 2

TELLING A PARABLE
FIGURE 5

temple to pray, one a Pharisee and the other a tax collector. The Pharisee stood and prayed thus with himself, 'God, I thank thee that I am not like other men, extortioners, unjust, adulterers, or even like this tax collector. I fast twice a week, I give tithes of all that I get.' But the tax collector, standing far off, would not even lift up his eyes to heaven, but beat his breast, saying, 'God, be merciful to me a sinner!' I tell you, this man went down to his house justified rather than the other; for every one who exalts himself will be humbled, but he who humbles himself will be exalted."

—Luke 18:9–14

The parable of the Pharisee and tax collector was spoken by Jesus "to some who trusted in themselves that they were righteous and despised others," to point out that entrance to the kingdom of heaven was not by good deeds but by the acceptance of God's grace. Grace, which is a beautiful gift of God, is not to be earned but can only be accepted as a present by those who know they do not deserve it, but nevertheless may accept it.

The Pharisee represents all the qualities of the Adapted Child. Knowledge and obedience to what is right and wrong, good and bad, what is pleasing to God and what is hateful to God, what "proves" righteousness and what is obviously unrighteousness, the law and lawlessness—all are evidences of the Adapted Child to reassure him that he is on the right track, going in the right direction, at the end of which he is going to deserve the favor and blessings of God.

The Pharisee, as the Adapted Child, collects brownie stamps. For each "good" thing he does or each "evil" he resists he knows he deserves a brownie stamp. Listen, as he enumerates his accomplishments:

"God I thank thee that I am not like other men:

extortioners	(1 brownie stamp)
unjust	(1 brownie stamp)
adulterers	(1 brownie stamp)
tax collector	(1 brownie stamp)
I fast . . .	(2 brownie stamps)
I give tithes"	(5 brownie stamps)

We can imagine him collecting brownie stamps and gleefully pasting them in his brownie stamp book. In time it would be full and he would redeem it for the prize he knew he deserved. His prayer life consisted of bringing himself up-to-date in the heavenly bookkeeping account, making certain that God was giving him the proper credit for his faithful service. After working for the company for a lifetime he knew he deserved a gold watch.

There is a very important word that separates the characters in the story. This is the little word but. This word brings people back to reality and reminds them that the Christian faith is not a religion of merit. The nuts and bolts of real Christianity is not what a person has done for himself but what God offers to give him in spite of his actions.

The tax collector, even in his spiritual poverty, recognizes that he deserves nothing, except to be rejected. As the Pharisee stood at the altar, the tax collector barely entered the door of the temple. The glances, the looks, the whispers, the verbals and the nonverbals of everyone in the temple including the professionals (in vestments and in the pews) all reminded him that he was undeserving. He still enters the temple and stands at the doorway. Smiting his chest he says, "God, be merciful to me a sinner." We can imagine that he feels he is unfaithful and undeserving and he knows it. His Adult tells him that he has no merits, no spiritual accomplishments, no "points," no brownie stamps. In fact, he even misplaced his brownie stamp book that he had received on his confirmation day. But he still recognizes his spiritual need to be forgiven and accepted by his creator and Lord. He knows enough to pray; he does not know enough to cite evidence of his goodness, only to say, "This is all I am; but I am honestly approaching your holiness and I merit nothing, unless you choose to claim me. But I am open, and honest, and willing, and trusting, and unprejudiced, and undeserving, and expecting, and pliable, and unsophisticated. I cast myself upon the mercy of the court. I am guilty, but I am willing to admit it. I am unashamed of my tears (Natural Child)."

Jesus says of this man, "I tell you, this man went down to his house justified (forgiven) rather than the other." I believe the difference is that the prayer of the Pharisee emanated from the Adapted Child in control, but the prayer of the tax collector came from the Natural Child (supervised by the Adult) in control. The Adult supervision made him stick to the facts rather than to fancy. He knew the facts, that he was unfaithful to God in that his life was not in accordance with the ten commandments, that sometimes violations took place willingly, that his life had hurt others as well as himself, and that his righteousness was as a "polluted garment," as Isaiah had learned many years before (Isaiah 64:6). He knew he had not been ethical in his relationships; he was a

Scrooge and Benedict Arnold to his countrymen. He had sold out to Caesar. He had his price and he was willing to be paid for it. He could not justify his motives, his action, his position, his sinfulness. He was hated by all, including the Romans to whom he made his regular payments. People could not tolerate him. He could not even tolerate himself. For these reasons he threw himself at the mercy of the court and was willing to accept any crumbs of mercy that might come his way. Of him, Jesus says, "This man was justified rather than the other." The determining feature is not that Jesus approved his morality or theology, but that he approached the throne of grace as a Natural Child while, the other man was trying to collect his reward as the Adapted Child.

This is a hard and very important lesson to be learned by a member of the "chosen race," a "New Testament or Old Testament Pharisee," or even a "Liberal Christian"—those whose religion is based upon saving brownie stamps or who rationally approach religion only through the intellect.

I find that the parable of the prodigal son illustrates several dimensions of human life, showing not only what happens to the Natural Child when it is not supervised by the Adult, but also its potential for fulfillment, resourcefulness and joy when it is under supervision. The parable also vividly shows the hangups, frustrations, and bitterness of the Adapted Child. Behind both of these "sons" there is a father who loves each one equally and desires that good come to both. His love is so great, however, that he gives them the freedom and responsibility to make their own choices (Figure 6).

And he said, "There was a man who had two sons; and the younger of them said to his father, 'Father, give me the share of property that falls to me.' And he divided his living between them. Not many days later, the younger son gathered all he had and took his journey into a far country, and there he squandered his property in loose living. And when he had spent everything, a great famine arose in that country, and he began to be in want. So he went and joined himself to one of the citizens of that country, who sent him into his fields to feed swine. And he would gladly have fed on the pods that the swine ate; and no one gave him anything. But when he came to himself he said, 'How many of my father's hired servants have bread enough and to spare, but I perish here with hunger! I will arise and go to my father, and I will say to him, "Father, I have sinned against heaven and before you;

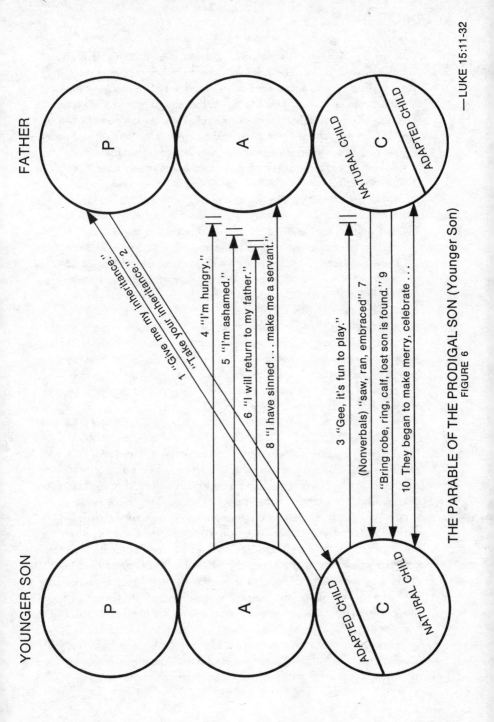

YOUNGER SON

FATHER

1 "Give me my inheritance."
2 "Take your inheritance."
3 "Gee, it's fun to play."
4 "I'm hungry."
5 "I'm ashamed."
6 "I will return to my father."
7 (Nonverbals) "saw, ran, embraced"
8 "I have sinned . . . make me a servant."
9 "Bring robe, ring, calf, lost son is found."
10 They began to make merry, celebrate . . .

THE PARABLE OF THE PRODIGAL SON (Younger Son)
FIGURE 6

—LUKE 15:11-32

I am no longer worthy to be called your son; treat me as one of your hired servants." ' And he arose and came to his father. But while he was yet at a distance, his father saw him and had compassion, and ran and embraced him and kissed him. And the son said to him, 'Father, I have sinned against heaven and before you; I am no longer worthy to be called your son.' But the father said to his servants, 'Bring quickly the best robe, and put it on him; and put a ring on his hand, and shoes on his feet; and bring the fatted calf and kill it, and let us eat and make merry; for this my son was dead, and is alive again; he was lost, and is found.' And they began to make merry.

"Now his elder son was in the field; and as he came and drew near to the house, he heard music and dancing. And he called one of the servants and asked what this meant. And he said to him, 'Your brother has come, and your father has killed the fatted calf, because he has received him safe and sound.' But he was angry and refused to go in. His father came out and entreated him, but he answered his father, 'Lo, these many years I have served you, and I never disobeyed your command; yet you never gave me a kid, that I might make merry with my friends. But when this son of yours came, who has devoured your living with harlots, you killed for him the fatted calf!' And he said to him, 'Son, you are always with me, and all that is mine is yours. It was fitting to make merry and be glad, for this your brother was dead, and is alive; he was lost, and is found.' "

—Luke 15:11–32

To paraphrase this story in the Transactional Analysis model would go something like this: A man had two sons. The younger son was motivated by the Natural Child who said to his father, "Let me have my share of the inheritance so that I may find my enjoyment now, in an intense way, while I am still young and able to enjoy it." Upon receiving these resources he went on a trip that took him to exciting places where he had a sensuous time. Temporary companions were attracted to his friendly nature and his unselfish spending of his money. He awoke one day to discover that he was without finances or friends. To make matters worse the country was suffering from famine of food and employment opportunities. To fill his stomach he took the only available job, which to a Jew was degrading and disgusting. He became a swinekeeper, a nursemaid to pigs. He had sunk so low that he had more in common with the pigs than he did with people. He even envied the animals in their ability to fill their stomachs with the pig food.

Suddenly his Adult took control and examined the facts. He was hungry, disillusioned, ashamed, and lonely. He remembered what it was like at home where even the servants had enough to eat. He made a decision to return home, and if need be, to become a servant to his father and brother. When he returned home, he discovered that he was still a son, loved by his father, and was restored to sonship. The celebration and reception given by the father at this time appealed to his Natural Child, but from this moment on his Adult made the decision that supervision of the Natural Child was necessary, not only to avoid waste, but to assure permanent and genuine happiness. This son was not really free until the Adult dimension liberated his Natural Child and then maintained supervision.

The older son was in the dimension of the Adapted Child (Figure 7). He always did the right thing. He was not like that no-good, spendthrift brother of his who degraded the family name. The Adapted Child always faithfully followed all the rules, and thus deserved many books of brownie stamps. Happiness to him was counting how many books of stamps he had saved, after the chores were over for the day. In the flickering shadows of the oil lamp he dreamed of his trip to the redemption center. One night when he came in from the fields to repeat this ritual, tired, hungry, and thirsty, he heard music, dancing, laughter, and gaiety. No one had invited him to a party. When he heard it was in honor of his brother, he was doubly angry. The father tried to share his happiness by saying, "Your brother is safely home." His answer was filled with the bitterness and wrath that only an Adapted Child knows. "I have always done what you asked, working my tail off every day. You never gave a party for me and I really am the one who deserves one. Yet you continued to waste resources on that no good son who wasted your money!"

He refused to share in the festivities, preferring to simmer in self-pity, and spent the rest of the evening pouting and complaining. He couldn't even find any enjoyment in counting his stamp books that night. He was unable to enjoy life because he possessed a "NOT OK" Child. He would have been miserable if he had gone to the party and his gloominess would have been out of place. In fact, he would probably not have been able to enjoy a party held in his honor as it would have distracted him from saving brownie stamps and ruined his great record of never having a party. This is the same motivation that some people feel when they boast that they haven't taken a vacation in X number of

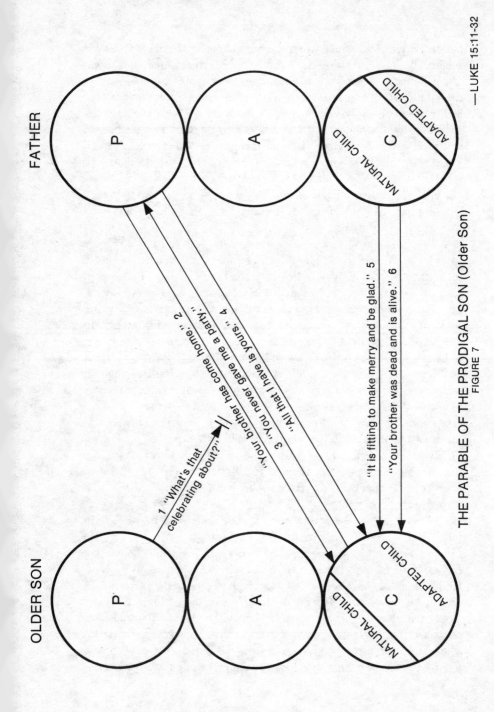

FATHER

OLDER SON

P

A

C

NATURAL CHILD

ADAPTED CHILD

P

A

C

NATURAL CHILD

ADAPTED CHILD

1 "What's that celebrating about?"

2 "Your brother has come home."

3 "You never gave me a party."

4 "All that I have is yours."

5 "It is fitting to make merry and be glad."

6 "Your brother was dead and is alive."

THE PARABLE OF THE PRODIGAL SON (Older Son)
FIGURE 7

—LUKE 15:11-32

years. To go on vacation would spoil their record and their boast of dedication.

This parable illustrates the kingdom of heaven and can only be appreciated by those who have an "OK" Child. The rest of the people will have a contempt for the hero of the story, sympathy for the position of the Adapted Child, and disgust for a father who was able to liberate his own Natural Child.

Not all the parables are as long and involved as these two illustrations. Many are short and to the point. Jesus talked of a merchant shopping for pearls; when he found one of great size, value, and prominence he sold all that he had to possess it (Matthew 13:45–46). He told of a fisherman throwing a net into the sea (Matthew 13:47ff), of a farmer sowing seeds (Matthew 13:3ff), a woman baking bread (Matthew 13:33), a treasure hidden in a field (Matthew 13:44), a house built on a rock (Matthew 7:24ff), a barren fig tree (Luke 13:6ff), a great banquet (Luke 14:15ff), laborers in a vineyard (Matthew 20:1ff), the marriage of a king's son (Matthew 22:1ff), and a Samaritan who was neighborly (Luke 10:29ff). Additional parables were told upon many different occasions, even to the point that every time Jesus spoke, he did so in parables. "All this Jesus said to the crowds in parables; indeed he said nothing to them without a parable. (Matt. 13:34)."

This caused the disciples to ask why he was so hung up on the parable method. His answer was to the point:

> To you it has been given to know the secrets of the kingdom of heaven, but to them it has not been given. For to him who has will more be given, and he will have abundance; but from him who has not, even what he has will be taken away. This is why I speak to them in parables, because seeing they do not see, and hearing they do not hear, nor do they understand.
>
> —Matthew 13:11–13

The parables had to be "felt" through the dimension of the Natural Child. It was through the senses that they had to be known. The reasoning process (Adult) was able to find some worthwhile materials in the parables, but the real message had to be "seen" and "heard" and "felt" through the Natural Child. Jesus spent much time with the disciples sharing this technique. He revealed this methodology of the kingdom to them. They knew the secret that opened heaven's gates. They and all others who could muster the Natural Child would be additionally blessed. "More would be given to them." But those who approached the parables through the Adult, and who had been able to receive a little understanding, "even what they had would be taken away," if they could not muster the Natural Child.

Quoting from the prophet Isaiah, Jesus continues:

"You shall indeed hear but never understand,
and you shall indeed see but never perceive.
For this people's heart has grown dull,
  and their ears are heavy of hearing,
  and their eyes they have closed,
lest they should perceive with their eyes,
  and hear with their ears,
and understand with their heart,
  and turn for me to heal them."
—Isaiah 6:9–10 quoted in Matthew 13:14ff

Then Jesus said to the disciples, "But blessed are your eyes, for they see, and your ears, for they hear (Matt. 13:16)."

Perhaps a better way of saying this would be, "But blessed are your eyes, *when* they see, and your ears, *when* they hear," because the disciples sometimes lacked the ability to use their Natural Child resources to feel the message of the kingdom (Matthew 13:36, 15:15). Finally Jesus said, "Are you also still without understanding (Matt. 15:16)?"

The key to understanding parables is in the area of "feeling" with the heart, "hearing" with the ears, "perceiving" with the eyes. The Christian faith is a "heart," not a "head" religion. It has to be felt, not logically grasped. It is not irrational, for the Adult supervises the Natural Child, but the ability to reason cannot of itself accept the invitation to share in the kingdom of God. A dull heart, like a dull knife, is not an effective tool. Conversion ("turn for me to heal them") is not a logical decision, carefully documented, rationally accepted. It is the response of the person in the dimension of the Natural Child to the loving invitation of the Natural Child of Jesus. And this response is as appropriate today as it was in the first century, for the invitation to share in the kingdom of heaven is open-ended, available to any who can receive it through the Natural Child.

Many persons in the first century recognized that the teaching of Jesus about religion and life was not through the traditional method of citing an authority, which included quoting the Law or a scholarly interpretation, but through fulfilling relationships. He was not detached from life and theology, objectively talking about God and man, but he got involved in the business of loving and responding to the love of God. His "authority" was a special kind of relationship that he shared with his Father, which has overtones that produced harmony in his relationship with his "brothers." Jesus knew the Law and the prophets and often quoted from these authorities. But when he did so it was not just to document his position but to recapture the "spirit" contained within the quotation. The prophets were not dead rocks to form into a solid foundation of a theological building, but living personalities whose "spirit" was ever present. The Law was not a tool to use on the heads of people, to beat them into believers and make them good people; instead, the "spirit" of the Law was alive and could be used to inspire people into loving relationships. He stated that he did not come "to destroy the Law," but "to fulfill it." He was not just obedient to the Law, limited by it, for he lived by the higher law, the law of love. Obedience is the motivation of the Adapted Child trying to please the Parent. Jesus' way was the Natural Child, supervised by the Adult, that responded to love. This relationship that he enjoyed was shared with those who could activate the Natural Child. Joy and abundant life became realities for all who responded in this way.

4

The Dimension in Jesus Called Parent

It is believed that the Parent dimension in a person is well established by the age of five or six. By this time certain authority figures make their indelible impression of right and wrong, the good and the bad, the acceptable and the unacceptable. This position is taken long before the Adult or rational side is able to filter out the truth from prejudice and half-truths. The material in the Parent is accepted as truth and often guides the person the rest of his life. Sometimes it is not even questioned, for it occupies a privileged spot closely identified with other "divine" revelations. Stored up in the Parental resources locker are the "do's" and "don'ts" of living. These injunctions are carefully carved in the rock of childhood to be preserved for future reference and direction. As these edicts are permanently recorded there are overtones of solemn and vivid emotion. When the information is recalled and applied, the emotions command obedience. Not only are the rules remembered but also the emotions accompanying the rules.

The Parent dimension motivates the Adapted Child, causing him to jump through all the required hoops of conduct. Obedience by the Adapted Child brings rewards (of brownie stamps to be pasted in the brownie stamp book) and hence the approval of the Parent. Disobedience by the Adapted Child causes the stamp collecting program to be temporarily interrupted and activates the full wrath of the Parent in judgment, producing feelings of guilt, inadequacy, and rejection, which are "NOT OK" feelings.

The Adapted Child feels "NOT OK." He never feels "OK." His only pleasure is to keep the Parent off his back and have some temporary relief from the Parent's criticism by saving stamps. Any satisfaction the Adapted Child obtains is counting his pages full of brownie stamps and anticipating his prize. The Parent keeps the Adapted Child feeling "NOT OK," for this is the only way strict observance of the rules can be assured.

Blessed is the person whose Parental injunctions are built upon the truth, where the Adult is able to reality-test the recorded regulations and not forced to remold or remake the rule book. Happy is the person whose Adapted Child does not have to lie prostrate before the demanding Parent, where the person sees himself as "OK" and the world about him as "OK." What a great world it would be if all people had an "I'M OK—YOU'RE OK" life-style, where Parental injunctions are evaluated by the Adult computer and are found to be consistent with other recorded data.

Before a person enters public school, while he is gathering material for his Parent dimension, he may feel "NOT OK." He is alert to criticism, inadequacies, and imperfections; he also learns how to please the authority figures without and the Parent within. He learns the value of brownie stamps and what is offered at the redemption center. His Parent directs him to save for a worthwhile prize. Through discipline, punishment, threats, and obedience he gathers Parental material for present conduct and future reference. One great handicap exists. Some of the information copied from the authority figures may not be true. In fact, it may be hurtful, antisocial and prejudiced. Abiding by this misinformation may bring brownie stamps, but it also may bring frustration, problems, and unhappiness.

For instance, it matters greatly to a little person what his authority figures teach about the police and civil law. If policemen are viewed with contempt, if law and order are disregarded and openly violated, these "facts" are observed by the little people and their Parent dimension will probably have contempt for civil authority. If the authority figures speak disparagingly of the church and organized religion, talk about the corruption, greed, sensuousness, and hypocrisy within the church, and view the clergy with suspicion, the little ones observe this data and store it for future reference. Sending the "kids" to Sunday school when the authority figures are neutral or antagonistic toward the church not only produces confusion in the minds of the little ones but causes them to record some strange materials in their Parent dimension. A sign outside a church building had in large letters, "DON'T SEND YOUR CHILDREN TO OUR SUNDAY SCHOOL" caused much concern among the people in the neighborhood. A closer look revealed small letters printed at the bottom of the sign which caused the message to make sense. The completing words were, "BRING THEM!" Sending children to Sunday school says one thing: bringing children to Sunday school says something else; refusing to let children go to Sunday school says something and ridiculing persons who go to Sunday school also makes its own point.

To test out the theory that little ones are affected by authority figures one is advised to observe them secretly as they "play house." Mothers and fathers are embarrassed to hear their own expressions, ideas, and hang-ups, when they take the time to overhear their children at play. The children play house just like Mommy and Daddy. They talk, act, swear, react just as they have observed Mommy and Daddy doing many times. When they grow up they will probably "play house" just as they learned earlier in the home. What seemed right when they were young will have the same significance when they are older. Mothers who scream at their children will probably raise children who scream at their children. Fathers who are critical of others but excuse their own mistakes will raise a similar breed. This is learned behavior and contained within the Parent.

It is also true that the Parent dimension has many constructive features. Vast amounts of materials are stored which save much time. When you drive your car and come to a traffic signal the Parent tells you the right thing to do automatically. You do not even have to think about it. A red light means "Stop," a green light means "Go." This was learned long before you learned to drive a car. Suppose that each time you came to an intersection you had to turn to the right place in the vehicle code book and then have a twenty-minute discussion with others in the car to determine your action; you would cause a serious traffic jam and be late for your commitments.*

The Parent is an important dimension in life. It speaks with authority. When this authority parallels Adult data, proper goals are reached, life has meaning and purpose. When its demands are at the expense of reason (Adult) and joy (Natural Child), the Adapted Child nervously follows its orders. Fear, frustration, guilt may result.

---

* The Adult *does* read the vehicle code and memorizes material not learned in childhood. The Adult also evaluates the traffic material in the Parent, makes needed corrections, turns the Parent off when necessary, and encourages the Natural Child as appropriate.

These points have application in the person of Jesus as well as in our own relationships. Jesus was raised in a home where discipline seemed to be undergirded with love. Since Mary and Joseph were of the Jewish faith there is little doubt that they were concerned about their offspring Jesus and that this concern must have been directed by many "do's" and "don'ts." The Jewish code of living contained 614 laws. These attempted to regulate every occasion, every situation, every transaction. When Jesus was eight days old he was circumcised, and later dedicated in the temple. The traditional approach to religion and ethical living were so intertwined that often they were seen as one and the same. There was a correct way of doing everything, from offering a sacrifice on the altar in the temple to cleansing the kitchen utensils or the hands in the home. What you did on certain days, what you refrained from doing on other days was legalistic directed. Steps taken on the sabbath day had to be counted carefully so that the maximum number be not exceeded and thus be considered work. There was a time for worship, for study, for work, for play. Probably these rules were taught in formal instruction classes at the knee of Mary and later in the synagogue. Although there was much discussion by traditionalists about the interpretation of the Law, for instance which law was the greatest, there was little opportunity to relax any of them. Legalism was not dependent upon private feelings. Every person was obligated to keep every law. This was the traditional religious and moral atmosphere of first-century Judaism.

The home, community, school, and synagogue were Parent-oriented. The law was to be memorized and followed. There were to be no exceptions. It was a comfortable environment for the Adapted Child as he learned right from wrong, good from bad, God's will versus man's will. Although learned men spent lifetimes in becoming legal specialists, the reverence for the law was learned by professional and layman at an early age. By keeping the law one pleased the Parent within and one's authority figures without, which included father, mother, rabbi, and God. Violations of the law brought stern judgment and swift punishment but also intense feelings of guilt and inferiority. A "NOT OK" feeling could have been a common experience, living in such a perfect and "OK" world.

God was pictured as not only executive, law maker, but also law enforcer: the president, the legislature, and the judiciary. He was understood as high and mighty but terribly concerned about the smallest infraction. Judgment and punishment were swiftly administered. The world shook, the lightening bolts came out of the black sky, there was fire and brimstone, sulphur, and ashes; the world and individuals hung in a precarious balance by a thin thread. The Adapted Child shook with fear when these images were contemplated. Only obedience could save a person or a nation from his wrath. A sacrificial system was inaugurated whereby blood could atone for blood, life for life, breath for breath. A victim must be consumed, the wrath had to be appeased; a scapegoat could be substituted; judgment demanded punishment, even if it meant the substitution of an innocent victim. It was believed that sins could be transferred from generation to generation. Children yet unborn would be punished for the misdeeds of the great-great grandparents. There was judgment, wrath, pain, sacrifice, blood, sweat, guilt, and atonement.

It is assumed that Jesus was raised in this traditional approach to life and religion. These images may have been indelibly stamped upon his Parent dimension, with his Adapted Child falling in step as he began saving brownie stamps and pasting them into the brownie stamp book along with his contemporaries. Yet, there was a spirit of love and openness in his life that went beyond keeping the jot and the tittle of the Law. Though he and his family followed the law they were not hung up on it. The spirit and the intention of the law must have been scrupulously evaluated by the Adult of Mary and Joseph, with a higher law, the law of love, being the motivation to devotion to God and ethical living. Living the law of love not only was a more fulfilling way of life but also produced desirable overtones in the relationship with God and fellowman. This loving atmosphere was ideal for raising a family and had a profound effect upon the firstborn son, Jesus. He knew the hang-ups and frustrations that the Adapted Child struggles with to please the authoritarian Parent within and the authority figures without. But he also knew the satisfaction and joy of the Natural Child under the supervision of the Adult. No doubt there must have been some criticism of the carpenter's home by those who kept the law of orthodoxy.

In reading the Gospel account there are a few times recorded where Jesus' Adult had to struggle with his Parent in order for the Natural Child to get and maintain liberation. The first of these struggles took place at the baptism of Jesus and then in the temptation struggle immediately following the baptism. The mission and message of John the Baptist was Parent-oriented and hit the hearer in the Adapted Child. "Get right with God, now!" "Repent!" "Be baptized!" "Judgment time has come!" His voice, his manner, his mission, his message all came through in a stern, demanding, judgmental way. There was no time for

Adult evaluation and discussion. When John preached he came through as a strong Parent. Listeners were hit in their "NOT OK" or Adapted Child. They must have felt small, inadequate, lost, and unworthy. They felt that they had to do something to get right with God. They listened, they were convicted of sin, they wept, they made promises, they followed the directions of John, they were baptized. Upon becoming baptized they got a brand new brownie stamp book and the motivation to begin the process of collecting stamps and pasting them in the book. Now they were right with God, and to keep right with God they had to work "to beat hell" and save as many stamps as possible, thus proving their devotion and discipleship.

John the Baptist was a traditionalist. His father, a "son" of Aaron, was a professional clergyman. John grew up in the parsonage. He lived in an ecclesiastical atmosphere. His father was a priest in the temple and he too was in the priestly line. His mother also was out of the priestly family, being "of the daughters of Aaron (Luke 1:5)." The priests were specialists in regard to the Law and its interpretation, religious worship (which included the sacrificial system and ministering in the temple), and morality. The priests were charged with safeguarding the purity of doctrine, ritual, ethical living, and obedience to God. They were the spiritual "fathers" of the people who devoted their entire lives to serving God by laboring in the temple. Special laws regulated the personal lives of the priests and their families. They were expected to be living examples of holiness and obedience. Religion was a twenty-four-hour-a-day, seven-days-a-week discipline. This discipline dictated conduct in the temple and in the home. The eyes of the community (and the Jewish world) were upon the priests, their wives, and their children. Any variations from orthodoxy were quickly noted by the adherents of the faith. Thus the priest and his family lived in a glass goldfish bowl, under the critical eyes of the law, the community, and the Parent dimension within.

This was the environment into which John was born. Although we know no details of his home life as a boy it can be assumed the house was "kosher" in orthodoxy and pietism. John probably received the best education and training that Judaism could provide. Being born to aged parents probably caused him to be in the spotlight during these early years. There was probably little time for fun and games. Satisfaction must have come to him in the form of praise for his spiritual progress, which meant the discipline of learning the Law with its interpretation and application, temple ritual, and moral application. The only game he could safely play in the home and community was that of playing temple much like the children of Protestant clergymen today play church.

Jesus and John were cousins. Although the hometown of Jesus was Nazareth, and the hometown of John was Jerusalem or one of its suburbs, they probably knew each other well in the growing up process. When they became young men, and John went to live in the wilderness, their contacts were probably less frequent. They had much in common; their religion, their family traditions, their social customs, their love of God and God's temple. Whereas Jesus became knowledgeable of the carpenter profession, and with it the related social activity with people, John went into the wilderness to live the life of an ascetic. He was a holy man. He soon gained the reputation of being a mystic and became the religious and social conscience of the people. He was recognized as God's man, a prophet who lived close to God and who called sinful persons back to God. People responded to his preaching. His ministry was not performed in the temple that he loved so much. He stayed near the Jordan River, where water was handy for the many baptisms he performed. Thus, he earned the title of John the Baptizer, or John the Baptist.

Why Jesus came to be baptized of John has been the subject of much discussion and reflection throughout the years. Did Jesus need to repent and believe? Did he need to get right with God? Did he need to be saved? Did he need to be reminded of his religious obligations to his fellowman? Did he need to have his sins forgiven? Which dimension of Jesus was present when he came to be baptized? Was it his Parent? Was it his Adult? Was it his "NOT OK" Child? Was it his "OK" Child?

Up to this point in John's ministry he came through as strong Parent to the Adapted Child of the people. There were threats. "Who warned you to flee from the wrath to come? . . . Even now the axe is laid to the root of the trees; every tree therefore that does not bear good fruit is cut down and thrown into the fire (Luke 3:7, 9)." When John was questioned about his mission and authority, whether he was the Messiah which was to come he had replied, "I baptize you with water; but he who is mightier than I is coming, the thong of whose sandals I am not worthy to untie; he will baptize you with the Holy Spirit and with fire (Luke 3:16)." Into this situation Jesus made his appearance. At first John was reluctant to baptize Jesus. After an Adult to Adult discussion on the subject, John went ahead and baptized Jesus. It was as though Jesus was saying to John, "I agree with what you are doing, and I submit myself to your ministry. I have come out of hiding and now am willing and ready to begin what I need to do." The baptism of Jesus by John was Adult-Adult. It was a rational acceptance of what John was doing and marks the official beginning of Jesus' ministry.

After the baptism Jesus went into the wilderness for meditation and reflection. I believe that an intense struggle took place between the Parent and the Adult of Jesus. This was the struggle of orthodoxy and rationality. In the conflict the Adult overpowered the Parent's demands for a traditional approach to religion. The basis of devotion to God and service to fellowman would be Adult oriented with the Natural Child liberated, rather than the Parent making the Adapted Child jump through the hoops of orthodoxy.

It was in the wilderness that Jesus came to grips with himself. Throughout his growing-up period in the home there must have been times when the Parent made its demands for traditionalism. In the wilderness, the conflict was vivid and powerful. It is pictured in the Gospels as a struggle between Satan and Jesus (Matthew 4:1ff, Mark 1:12–13, Luke 4:1ff). In Hebrew thought, evil was personified as Satan, the devil, the tempter. I believe this was really part of the Parent dimension and in reality it was a struggle of the Parent trying to sway the Adapted Child, but the Adult of Jesus maintained control and eventually silenced the Parent (i.e., Satan).

Scripture was quoted by both the Parent and Adult: Three victories were won by the Adult; the Parent was silenced. Throughout the life and ministry of Jesus, the Parent was kept under heavy control by the Adult. Only a few times would the Parent be able to wrest control. These times will be discussed later in this chapter.

The first "temptation" was that of physical need.

> Then Jesus was led up by the Spirit into the wilderness to be tempted by the devil. And he fasted forty days and forty nights, and afterward he was hungry. And the tempter came and said to him, "If you are the Son of God, command these stones to become loaves of bread." But he answered, "It is written, 'Man shall not live by bread alone, but by every word that proceeds from the mouth of God.'"
>
> —Matthew 4:1–4

What is more necessary than bread when a man is hungry? And Jesus was truly hungry. The devil (Parent) came on strong, "Command these stones." The stones in the desert must have looked like loaves of bread, and the Parent was determined to swerve him from his real mission of revealing the truth about God and man. But the Adult of Jesus took command and said, "There is something more important in life than bread." The ability to know the facts of the kingdom of God, the word of God, and to be able to enjoy it far outweighed the short-term desire for something miraculous to eat. Truth is more important than bread.

The second temptation (through the Parent dimension) that Jesus squarely met with his Adult was in the realm of the dramatic, the magical.

> Then the devil took him to the holy city, and set him on the pinnacle of the temple, and said to him, "If you are the Son of God, throw yourself down; for it is written, 'He will give his angels charge of you,' and 'On their hands they will bear you up, lest you strike your foot against a stone.' " Jesus said to him, "Again it is written, 'You shall not tempt the Lord your God.' "
>
> —Matthew 4:5–7

Again the direction of the devil (Parent) gave a strong order, "Cast yourself down!"

To be able to defy the laws of nature would in the end produce disorder and chaos. The Adult in Jesus could see the fallacy of trying to manipulate the law of gravity to one's own end. He could gain a reputation but in the process he would become ineffective in living and working with people in a disorganized universe. The Adult in Jesus rejected the offer to possess magical powers that would set him apart from humanity. He rejected the offer to be a "superstar."

The third temptation was one that many persons had succumbed to before. This was in the realm of power and wealth.

> Again, the devil took him to a very high mountain, and showed him all the kingdoms of the world and the glory of them; and he said to him, "All these I will give you, if you will fall down and worship me." Then Jesus said to him, "Begone, Satan! for it is written, 'You shall worship the Lord your God and him only shall you serve.' " Then the devil left him, and behold, angels came and ministered to him.
>
> —Matthew 4:8–11

The last temptation was loaded. To be able to control wealth and men must indeed have been attractive and challenging. "All the kingdoms of the world" with the power and prestige that went with them was the offer by the devil (Parent) appealing to the Adapted Child. This temptation was not subtle in the least, but the Adult in Jesus recognized that the kingdoms of this world were a poor substitute for the kingdom of God. With great courage and insight the Adult of Jesus not only rejected the offer but also the one who made it.

The victory was final. The Adult was in control. Hence he was free to begin his ministry of sharing the secrets of the kingdom of God and making the kingdom accessible to men. Now the Natural Child could be liberated, to share the emotions of the kingdom of God. From this moment on the Adult of Jesus would stay in control (with only several exceptions), preventing further attacks from the Parent within or the devil without. Motivation for him and his friends would no longer be "fear" of God but "love" of God. Concern for the needs of men would no longer be legally dictated, causing the Adapted Child to collect brownie stamps for doing good; now concern for men would be out of love, not guilt.

Could it be that the struggle within Jesus is the same one other humans have to face? James 1:14 states: "Each person is tempted when he is lured and enticed by his own desire." This suggests that the struggle is within a person. When this happens, unless the Adult dimension is in control, the person may fall a victim. Paul counseled, "Put on the whole armor of God, that you may be able to stand against the wiles of the devil (Eph. 6:11)." Only the Adult can defend against the attack, whether it comes from within or without. "Resist the devil and he will flee from you (Jas. 4:7)."

The "NOT OK" or Adapted Child is afraid to examine the facts of the temptations of Jesus. The Natural Child not only has feelings about the struggle but "understands." Making bread of stones, standing on the pinnacle of the temple, contemplating the total wealth and power of the world whets the appetite and attention of the Natural Child. He glories in the language and imagery of the encounter. He breathlessly awaits the developments and the outcome. He is aware of the truth that develops and the victory that results. To the Natural Child, Jesus is the knight in shining armor that slays the dragon and receives the prize. The temptation scene is a parable of the kingdom of God to the Natural Child, feeling confident of the victory because the Adult is in control.

When Jesus accepted the "I'M OK—YOU'RE OK" position great things happened for mortals. No doubt he could have used the traditional approach to make people religious by saving brownie stamps as so many leaders had tried previously. But what makes Jesus unique and challenging is that he came to grips with the struggle that faced men. He assured us of the final victory, and promised joy and fulfillment in and after the struggle. To Jesus, the kingdom of God was not seen as a far-off tasteless place, but as a reality to be enjoyed in this life, extending into the life to come. The symbol for the kingdom is a cross, not a cushion; and it is a symbol of victory, not defeat.

There are several examples of Jesus' momentarily losing control by his Adult, and the Parent's taking over. These passages of scripture are often ignored or overlooked by Christians. Those who attempt to deal with them often rationalize and give excuses for his conduct. These situations are a strange contrast to the usual approach and manner of Jesus. Rather than destroy his image, some persons find it easier to identify with a spiritual leader who, like them, has "feet of iron and clay." He could, like us, in a moment of weakness lose control; the Parent and "NOT OK" Child anxiously await these moments so they can make their presence and desires known. When the Parent or "NOT OK" Child calls the shots, strange courses are steered and strange words are spoken. Let us turn to these accounts and face them in the model of Transactional Analysis.

> And behold, a Canaanite woman from that region came out and cried, "Have mercy on me, O Lord, Son of David; my daughter is severely possessed by a demon." But he did not answer her a word. And his disciples came and begged him, saying, "Send her away, for she is crying after us." He answered, "I was sent only to the lost sheep of the house of Israel." But she came and knelt before him, saying, "Lord, help me." And he answered, "It is not fair to take the children's bread and throw it to the dogs." She said, "Yes, Lord, yet even the dogs eat the crumbs that fall from their master's table." Then Jesus answered her, "O woman, great is your faith! Be it done for you as you desire." And her daughter was healed instantly.
>
> —Matthew 15:22–28

This situation happened in Gentile territory among non-Jewish persons. When Jesus was traveling incognito and happened to lodge at a local residence, the word got out that an important person was in town. Though his Parental mission was seen as ministering to "the lost sheep of the house of Israel" he sometimes was required to travel through

Gentile territory and deal with non-Jewish personnel. Frequently he was rejected in these places for the people sometimes cared more for their pigs than they did for religion or the needs of their fellowmen. "And behold, all the city came out to meet Jesus; and when they saw him, they begged him to leave their neighborhood (Matt. 8:34)." In addition he rarely was able to perform a physical or spiritual miracle in these Gentile areas, due to the lack of faith of the people.

Notice the nonverbals of the woman: "came out," "cried," "knelt," "begged." These all suggest the dimension of the Adapted or "NOT OK" Child. "Have mercy on me, O Lord, Son of David," she cried with great emotion. The nonverbal that Jesus returned was to ignore her and her request. She then went to the disciples who also were upset by her tactics. She really "bugged" the disciples. "Get her off our backs, Jesus," they said. His answer was cruel, "I was sent only to the lost sheep of the house of Israel." Jewish pride and prejudice came out from the Parent dimension of Jesus. But she came back again, this time kneeling and said, "Lord, help me." This triggered another cruel statement from the Parent dimension of Jesus. Perhaps it is the most painful statement he ever made. One can hardly imagine Jesus ever saying such a thing as, "It is not fair to take the children's bread and throw it to the dogs." But he did say it and rather than ignore the statement or omit it from the Gospel account, we need to see that this is a dimension of Jesus. This is the Parent dimension. It is judgmental, harsh, prejudiced, aloof, dogmatic, critical, degrading, hurtful, and unloving. This brought about a response from the Adult dimension of the woman. "Yes, Lord, yet even the dogs eat the crumbs that fall from their master's table." This was a fact. This was data. This was probably said without emotion. She literally said, "Let's just look at the facts." At the same time her faith came through in the double message. From the sound of it, the transaction was Adult-Adult. But the real message was Natural Child-Natural Child. This is the habitation of faith. It is supervised by the Adult. Jesus responded from his Natural Child, "O woman, great is your faith! Be it done for you as you desire!" The analysis of this confrontation is that at first both Jesus and the disciples came on strong as Parent. Later, Jesus shifted to Natural Child, and then performed a miracle.

The last few days before Jesus was crucified were not without frustration and uncertainty. After the Palm Sunday experience where Jesus was ushered into the holy city of Jerusalem as a king, seated on the back of a donkey, several illustrations of the Parent dimension are recorded. The first was the cursing of the fig tree.

> On the following day, when they came from Bethany, he was hungry. And seeing in the distance a fig tree in leaf, he went to see if he could find anything on it. When he came to it, he found nothing but leaves, for it was not the season for figs. And he said to it, "May no one ever eat fruit from you again." And his disciples heard it. . . . As they passed by in the morning, they saw the fig tree withered away to its roots. And Peter remembered and said to him, "Master, look! The fig tree which you cursed has withered."
>
> —Mark 11:12–14, 20–21

Coming from an overnight stay at Bethany, approaching the city of Jerusalem he was filled with thoughts of what must be done about the degeneration of temple worship and commercialism, the powerful opposition of the religious hierarchy and fickleness of the populace. In addition to these facts he was hungry. A lonely fig tree received his attention. This is the only miracle ever recorded in the Gospels that was performed by Jesus in a haphazard or damaging way. The text clearly states that it was not the season for figs. With his Parent in control he blasted, "May no one ever eat fruit from you again." The disciples were shocked at this statement and must have been bewildered by the curse he put on the tree. Later Peter reminded Jesus about what he had done, when they saw the withered tree on the return trip. The truth of this historic situation is that for a moment Jesus lost control by his Adult, and his Parent blasted a poor, innocent fig tree.

A similar incident happened in Jerusalem soon after the cursing of the fig tree.

> And they came to Jerusalem. And he entered the temple and began to drive out those who sold and those who bought in the temple, and he overturned the tables of the money-changers and the seats of those who sold pigeons; and he would not allow any one to carry anything through the temple.
>
> —Mark 11:15–16

John 2:15 gives the additional information that he made "a whip of cords, he drove them all, with the sheep and the oxen, out of the temple." Thus the merchants and those who bought their sacrificial coins and animals were literally driven out of the temple with the bitter words, "Is it not written, 'My house shall be called a house of prayer for all the nations'? But you have made it a den of robbers (Mark 11:17)." Great emotion is being shown here in action and word. He was demanding, critical, judgmental, authoritarian. His Parent, set in concrete at an early age, and reinforced by experiences throughout his life, reverenced and valued the temple and the priesthood. But man had profaned the sacred place, and the ecclesiastical authority had tolerated it; sharp action had to be taken. He did it with violent emotion and action. The Parent of Jesus was in control for another brief moment and no doubt convinced the authorities that this man was dangerous: he must be punished, he must be destroyed.

Later, when his authority was questioned he responded from the Parent dimension, to list a whole series of denunciations upon the scribes and Pharisees. He called them "hypocrites," "blind guides," "blind fools," "blind men," "like whitewashed tombs, which outwardly appear beautiful, but within they are full of dead men's bones and all uncleanness," "full of hypocrisy and iniquity," "you serpents," "you vipers (Matt. 23:1–36)." These are odd words coming from the lips of the prince of peace, who normally was full of compassion, forgiving, and understanding. It is a strange contrast to his stories of the kingdom (parables) and his statements about becoming "peacemakers."

But one can understand that sometimes even Jesus became emotional when his Parent dimension took over and consequently he came out with some fiery words and actions. Rather than detracting from his credentials of being the Son of God and savior of men, these happenings can cause people to identify more closely with him in his "humanness." He is just like one of us.

5

The Adult in Jesus

O God, give me the serenity
   to accept what cannot be changed—
Give me the courage to change what can be changed—
And the wisdom to know the one from the other.

                      —Reinhold Niebuhr

This beautiful prayer points out the necessity for a person to deal with life in a positive way, to take control rationally; to look at the facts of reality; to set realistic goals; to make choices based upon logic; and to assume the responsibility and consequences of the decisions, even in the face of threat and torture. The person who faces life with the Adult dimension in control will be motivated to use every available resource including divine assistance, and for this reason would turn to God for additional strength and wisdom. Jesus is a beautiful example of this dedication and self-control, for in nearly every circumstance (the few exceptions are discussed in the chapter "The Dimension In Jesus Called Parent") Jesus maintained control because his Adult was calling the shots. Jesus knew the secret to a satisfying, fulfilling, and fruitful life. This quality of life is available to anyone who is willing to look for and accept facts, and to silence the Parent within, whenever the inputs of the Parent are inappropriate or harmful.

When a person reads the New Testament account he is impressed that the characters in these historical situations are not pictured as superhuman, nor are they whitewashed in an attempt to cover up their blemishes. Their anxieties, fears, tempers, problems, weaknesses, uncertainties, doubts are all honestly faced. The reader becomes involved in their struggles because these biblical personages faced many of the same types of problems and situations that we face today. We have the advantages in that we can learn from their victories as well as their defeats. In the same way we can also learn a great deal from Jesus in his life and teaching. Jesus had a strong faith in God and was motivated to doing the will of God. This was undergirded by logically facing the facts, making decisions and then rationally facing the consequences of these decisions.

A decision that is based on logic and facts (Adult) can be lived with and worked through. Choices motivated either by authority ("This is what you must do" Parent) or fun ("Gee, let's play" Child) can cause uncertainty and its companions, regret and despair. The Adult in Jesus maintained control over both the Parent and Child dimensions and kept their inputs and motivations appropriate. The Christian religion as taught and lived by Jesus is a heart religion (Natural Child) supervised by the head (Adult). The Adult evaluates customs, traditions, legalism (Parent) as well as the counterparts—obedience, fear, anxiety (Adapted Child). Only when truth is considered and appropriate goals are established, can the Natural Child be liberated to enjoy life. But there can be some satisfaction in the dimension of the Adult, when data are considered and goals are reached, when one knows he is "on course" and in control.

Jesus was a disciplined man. Like an athlete who trains for a physical confrontation, so Jesus used every helpful resource to make him strong and valiant. Those who picture him as meek and mild, with a soft voice and effeminate mannerisms do him and his cause a real disservice. Jesus was a man. He was not a sissy, nor a ninety-pound weakling. Bullies did not kick sand in his face at the beach. He was a man among men. His real strength was not in his ability to excel in the olympic events of his day, but in his ability to do what was necessary even if it meant risking personal safety. The Adult dimension in control gave him "guts" in the face of conflict and trial, as well as fortitude in the environment of easy living. He had the serenity to face any situation and maintain control and direction.

This fortitude had its roots in the fact that Jesus was right with God and with his fellowman. He saw himself as an "OK" person in an "OK" world. Decisions were based upon logic. The facts were constantly being evaluated. He had a realistic attitude toward the world. He made responsible decisions and stood ready to face the consequences of his decisions, which is the final test of the Adult dimension.

Excuses and/or rationalizations were not part of his vocabulary or personality. Even when facing an obvious miscarriage of justice at his trial—where there were make-believe charges, false witnesses, bribery of the court, corruption of high officials, betrayal by friends, denial by associates, abandonment by his followers—he remained firm in his decisions and never once complained that his rights were being violated or that he was not getting a fair trial. Can you imagine his crying out, "I'm going to get a lawyer to defend me"; or "I'm not getting a fair shake"; or "I plead the Fifth Amendment"; or "This is a gross miscarriage of justice"; or "I'm innocent and I'll prove it by taking it all the way to the supreme court"; or "I was framed"; or "The judicial system is corrupt"; or "No one can get a fair trial here"; or "It's because I'm a Jew that they're picking on me"; or "I'll take a lie detector test to prove my innocence"; or "Anti-semitism!" or "The governor is a fink"; or "The high priest has sold out to Rome"; or "I'll tell my Father on you"; or "This is a smear campaign"; or "Politics are being played here"; or "Innuendos, half-truths, and smears"; or "Poppycock!"

The above statements are absurd when one considers the personality of Jesus. When he set his face to go to Jerusalem he was motivated by logic and data. He knew that he had enemies and they would stop at nothing to try to silence him. This was the Adult, not the Adapted Child who was to get fifty brownie stamps for a crucifixion.

He seemed unconcerned with accusations that he violated the sacred law of the Jews. Consistently the approach of Jesus was that people are more important than minute obedience to the Law. Thus when he and the disciples were hungry and were walking through the grain fields on the sabbath, they picked some of the wheat, rubbed it between their hands to remove the chaff, and ate the sweet nut-flavored seeds (Matthew 12:1–8). This was considered to be work by the traditionalists. Going into the synagogue there was a man with a deformed hand; Jesus healed him on the sabbath (Matthew 12:9–13). Again he was accused of violating the sabbath as his healing efforts were considered to be work and should have been done on days other than the sabbath. Jesus told them that he was liberating the man in the same way a farmer would liberate an animal if the animal got hung up on a fence or fell into a pit on the sabbath. It was logical that a man was worth more than an ox or a sheep.

He and his disciples were often accused of not ceremonially purifying themselves before they ate (Matthew 15:1ff), nor did they fast as did other faithful Jews (Matthew 9:15). Jesus' answer was that although there was some value to customs and traditions, there was a better motivation for living than just blindly following the accepted norms. It was expedient that these traditions be relaxed since the Messiah was present; here was an opportunity for new teaching and new examples of living, which were more important than legalism.

Jesus was constantly subjected to "loaded" questions, motivated by the desire of people not to learn and mature but to put him in an embarrassing position where his statements could be used against him. "Is it lawful to divorce one's wife for any cause (Matt. 19:3)?" "By what authority are you doing these things, and who gave you this authority (Matt. 21:23)?" "Is it lawful to pay taxes to Caesar, or not (Matt. 22:17)?" "If a man dies, having no children, his brother must marry the widow, . . . in the resurrection, whose wife will she be (Matt. 22:23; Mark 12:23)?" "Teacher, which is the great commandment in the law (Matt. 22:36)?" "Who is my neighbor (Luke 10:29)?" In each case the question was rationally answered even though the evil motivation behind the question was recognized. The Adult dimension of Jesus honestly and squarely faced these questions and logical data were generated, even though a slip of the tongue could have brought serious charges of blasphemy, conspiracy, and treason.

The teaching of Jesus is found throughout the four Gospels but a synopsis of his message and method can be found in the section of Matthew, chapters five through seven, commonly referred to as the Sermon on the Mount, a compilation of scattered materials assembled into one unit. This fertile seedbed of rational gems has been the motivation for many speeches, sermons, addresses, and quotations. The parables and the miracles appeal to the Natural Child under the supervision of the Adult. The content and approach here generally is Adult to Adult. This is the kind of material that can be used in data processing. This can be analyzed, discussed, dissected, and debated. However, the collection of data begins with a section commonly called the Beatitudes which speaks of true blessedness or happiness in terminology that appeals to the Natural Child.

The Beatitudes describe the feelings of the Natural Child testing a right relationship with God. Other sections of the Sermon on the

Mount which speak of the "kingdom of heaven," "your Father in heaven," "your Father," appeal to the relationship of the Natural Child with his heavenly Father. Similarly the terminology of the Lord's Prayer quoted in the Sermon on the Mount is in the imagery and language that is "understood" by the Natural Child, supervised by the Adult.

Other sections of the Sermon on the Mount, however, give logical direction on many subjects which include: murder (5:21–22), being summoned to appear in court (5:25–26), adultery (5:27–30), divorce (5:31–32), oath-taking (5:33–37), dealing with evil (5:38–42), perfection (5:48), giving alms (6:2–4), fasting (6:16–18), earthly treasure (6:19–21), loyalty (6:24), judging others (7:1–5), asking, seeking, finding (7:7–12), and testing false prophets (7:15–20). In these sections Jesus seems to be saying that the traditional legal approach is not sufficient for his people. You must use the gray matter God has given you properly to live your life. This dimension in life comes not by obedience but by choice, based upon facts and data. "Not every one who says to me, 'Lord, Lord,' shall enter the kingdom of heaven, but he who does the will of my Father who is in heaven (Matt. 7:21)." The key to learning the will of God and its application is faithful study which results in appropriate action and living. The mind does control our conduct toward others, whether this is in regard to assaulting them, taking advantage of them, stealing their property, abusing their names, violating their wives, judging their conduct, living as neighbors, and as fellow humans. The mind also directs our actions concerning God, as we give alms, make oaths, strive for perfection, fast, pray, and determine loyalty. A man's mind should control a man's body. Like the intricate movement in a fine watch, the mind is a delicate instrument which gives direction and health to the personality. A man never rises above his thoughts, for soon his thoughts find arms and legs. The book of Proverbs states, "As a man thinks . . . so is he (23.7, KJV)." The mind generates "evil thoughts, murder, adultery, fornication, theft, false witness, slander. These are what defile a man (Matt. 15:19–20)."

How do you deal with anxiety? How do you approach the subject of what to eat, drink, wear? What do you do about bodily needs? Jesus counsels us to put the Adult in control, face the facts, deal with data; but above all realize that your physical needs are no different from those faced by others. Is it possible to be prudent about your needs yet not be anxious? Is it possible to deal realistically with the basic needs of man without being unduly concerned? The answer is "Yes."

It is true that many people go to bed at night after living a day with a minimum or subminimum supply of food. The problem seems to be one of distribution, not supply. But to many persons who have more food than they need, even more calories than they can use, the counsel is not to be anxious about their own needs. Jesus already has given direction that we should share our resources, talents, and abilities. But what about our own needs? Jesus states, "Do not be overly concerned. Do not worry unduly about them." By being anxious you can neither grow taller nor add years to your life; excessive concern can be of little help in these issues. Here are the facts as found in Matthew 6:25ff: (1) Everyone has needs; (2) God made us (as well as other animals) with basic needs to exist, develop, and mature; (3) living is more than what we eat, drink, wear; (4) the birds have enough to eat, and yet they are not unduly concerned; (5) you are worth more than the birds; (6) worry cannot extend your life—it may even shorten it; (7) foolish people are overly concerned about the nonessentials of life; (8) put first things first: the kingdom of heaven is worth possessing for in it all the basic needs are satisfied with the bonus of joy and fulfillment; (9) if your life has the proper (Adult) direction, the essentials will be available also. Put first things first, and you will not be needful or sorry.

A religion or ethical system that ignores the discipline of the Adult dimension is programed for disaster if the Child calls the shots, and for frustration if the Parent is the motivator. The teaching of Jesus in these important areas is solidly rooted in the Adult. There is no blessing in stupidity or ignorance. He never required blind acceptance of doctrine or creed to prove orthodoxy or piety, nor did he legislate a standard code of conduct for moral living. His approach was based on fact and logic which would not disintegrate when persons honestly examined beliefs with reason. The Great Commandment was based on the test of "heart, soul, *mind*, and strength." The test of the "mind" is logic, and logic is the motivator and tool of the Adult dimension.

Jesus taught that it is difficult for a rich man to be content since his money may become his "god" and contaminate his outlook on life (Matthew 19:23ff). It is not riches that program a man to selfishness and greed but his attitude toward the riches. Money is not the basis of evil, but "The love of money is the root of all evils (1 Tim. 6:10)." There are other human factors that cause distortions in thinking and motivation. These factors are not detrimental in themselves, in fact they may indeed be assets. But one's attitude toward them makes them helpful or hurtful. It depends upon whether reason and logic are in control.

Within this area are such things as property, possessions, a wife, a husband, a son, a daughter, a family, real estate, commerce, military service, traditions, and customs. None of these important areas of living should distract a person from reaching goals logically determined by the Adult. The motivation that sets goals and keeps a man on course is his Adult dimension which looks at "facts" about earth and heaven, man and God.

Jesus, in the Adult dimension, used logic to prepare his disciples and himself for the facts of the crucifixion and the resurrection. He made prior announcements about his impending passion: "From that time Jesus began to show his disciples that he must go to Jerusalem and suffer many things from the elders and chief priests and scribes, and be killed, and on the third day be raised (Matt. 16:21)." Listen to the reaction of Peter, "God forbid, Lord! This shall never happen to you (16:22)." Jesus let Peter know that when he could not keep his Adult in control and face facts, he was actually a "hindrance" to him.

Another time he took the disciples aside as they were on the way to Jerusalem and he said, "Behold, we are going up to Jerusalem; and the Son of man will be delivered to the chief priests and scribes, and they will condemn him to death, and deliver him to the Gentiles to be mocked and scourged and crucified, and he will be raised on the third day (Matt. 20:18–19)."

This was the direction in which he was heading. The facts all pointed to the kind of treatment he was to face in Jerusalem. Jesus knew that he would be ridiculed, assaulted, falsely charged, tried, convicted, and then be killed in the traditional way that criminals were executed: crucifixion. But he also had the datum that God would be with him throughout the events. As man would write "The End" to the events of the crucifixion, God would write "To Be Continued" above man's statement. This was not a whistling in the dark, a grim stoic outlook, nor a martyr or hero complex. This was a faith undergirded with logic and fact. The Adult was in control, even when he faced crucifixion.

Jesus' teaching, though not set in complicated words and phrases, was profound. He had the ability to get right to the "nitty-gritty" without being wordy. He did not need to waste time trying to impress people with his great understanding and insights. He used simple expressions to teach interpersonal relationships and theological truths—a sign of greatness. "So whatever you wish that men would do to you, do so to them; for this is the law and the prophets (Matt. 7:12)."

Here is the "golden rule" to follow. Figure out rationally how you would like to be treated, and then treat people in the same way. When you judge others, you will be judged by your own standards. The way you forgive will be the way others and God will forgive you. The measuring unit you use for others will be used by them to measure your life. Life is serious business, not to be wasted by unplanned efforts. Use your head. Plan ahead. Look at the facts. Put your Adult in control. Make responsible decisions and then accept the consequences. This is the style of Jesus, and it is a guide for people today.

A good definition of sin is "to miss the mark." This can happen when we willingly or unconsciously miss the marks we have set for ourselves. The Adult knows when we have misused our energy and resources, when our lives are unproductive and hurtful. It is the Adult who must determine what is important in life, how we are going to reach it, and when we fail. The Adult keeps us moving in the right direction, utilizing every resource available, while giving feedback concerning our progress.

The life of Jesus is an example as to what potential can be realized within a person if Adult resources are used; but, in addition, when a person does not have to waste time in masquerading or projecting an image, he can get down to the fundamentals and achieve far-reaching accomplishments. In addition, the emphasis is upon the positive approach rather than the negative.

Recently a young couple who felt they were missing a dimension in marriage came to a counselor for some handles. It was determined by the wife after several sessions that the husband and wife should exchange lists of what bothered each about the words and actions of the mate. It was suggested by the counselor that each already was aware of negatives and shortcomings. Perhaps they should make a list of the positive and good qualities of the mate, which would be more important. When this was mentioned it was obvious to all present that it had been some time since the husband and the wife had mentioned what positive things they valued in their mates. An exchange of the constructive aspects of their personalities could not only produce some interesting data to be considered, but would reverse the trend to think negatively about one another.

Jesus was able to deal with the positive dimensions of life. He lived a sinfree life (viz., not missing the mark), not so much in that he possessed superpowers which normal mortals do not possess, but in that his Adult was so much in control, he was not swerved from his commitments and goals. Jesus had no supernatural abilities that his disciples of the first century and we do not also possess. The one ingredient that he used to such advantage was that his Adult was the controlling force in his life. This dimension was effective in assembling data and making appropriate choices and decisions, and also in having a basis for evaluating his Parent. When Parental inputs interfered with the facts they were silenced. In this environment the Natural Child of Jesus and those of his believers were encouraged to make their presence known and enjoy the benefits of the kingdom of heaven on earth without fear of attack from the Parent within or authority figures without. In this way the Natural Child lived in the sunshine of love, joy, and peace which are so important in this life and in the life to come.

This technique, these resources, these benefits are offered to all peopled who desire to take control with the Adult and then to liberate the (Natural) Child. Not everyone who had a confrontation with the Adult and Natural Child dimensions of Jesus responded in an affirmative way. Sometimes, even young people were unable to free their Child. Mark 10:17–22 describes the reaction of a young man of great potential:

> And as he was setting out on his journey, a man ran up and knelt before him, and asked him, "Good Teacher, what must I do to inherit eternal life?" And Jesus said to him, "Why do you call me good? No one is good but God alone. You know the commandments: 'Do not kill, Do not commit adultery, Do not steal, Do not bear false witness, Do not defraud, Honor your father and mother.' " And he said to him, "Teacher, all these I have observed from my youth." And Jesus looking upon him loved him, and said to him, "You lack one thing; go, sell what you have, and give to the poor, and you will have treasure in heaven; and come, follow me." At that saying his countenance fell, and he went away sorrowful; for he had great possessions.

A discussion took place between the Adult dimensions of the young man and Jesus. The young man was able to transact from the dimensions of the Parent, Adult, Adapted Child. But when Jesus invited him to discipleship from the Natural Child dimension, the young man "went away sorrowful; for he had great possessions." His resources prevented the liberation of his Natural Child. Consequently, he missed his entrance into the kingdom of heaven, which can only be entered through the dimension of the Natural Child. This is true for any person living in any century.

6

The Early Church
and the Liberated Child

The primary quality seen in the primitive church is that of the Natural Child responding to an experience. Converts to the faith were made in the dimension of the Natural Child, under the influence of Jesus (before and after his resurrection and ascension), the Holy Spirit, the apostles, or other Christian believers. The church of the first century went by the name of "The Way." Persons sharing the faith referred to the brotherhood as "saints," "brothers," "disciples," "believers." The first record of believers being called "Christians" was at Antioch where conversions were independent of the Jewish law. Love was the motivation of those who had found "The Way"; love of God as reflected by Jesus and the Holy Spirit, and love of each other as a family member of the household of faith.

One distinct feature of this early period was "the love feasts." These contained some elements of a modern-day "pot luck" church supper but had overtones of the eucharist. It must have reminded the ancient people not only of the Lord's Supper, as commissioned by Jesus, but also the many common meals he had shared with the disciples and other believers before the crucifixion. That abuse crept into the early church, under the liberation of the Natural Child without Adult supervision, is seen in the love feasts becoming a time of gluttony and drunkenness (1 Corinthians 11:20–22) where the widows and other needy persons were neglected (Acts 6:1). Other blemishes on the character of the church came about when the Natural Child of believers was unsupervised. These will be discussed later in this chapter.

One is impressed with the enthusiasm and naiveté of these first believers. They were open to new experiences, filled with a sense of wonder and expectancy, sensuous, responsive, self-abandoned, unprejudiced, intimate, unsophisticated, straightforward, spontaneous, happy. They were filled with the kind of joy that Jesus talked about and personified. They felt "OK" with God and with their fellowman. They sold all their property and put the proceeds into a common fund. They worshiped God daily, sometimes going to the temple in Jerusalem, sometimes participating in synagogue worship, but more often having informal religious services in homes and fields. They sang songs, hymns and spirituals, they laughed, they prayed, they ate together, they wept together, they witnessed together, they expected miracles of faith to happen, they saw wonders and signs that the kingdom of heaven was present in their midst, they experienced ecstasy in living. Life was beautiful, living was meaningful, religion was fulfilling, God was a natural reality. These are all the qualities of the liberated Natural Child; these persons had found a quality of life that was fulfilling and exciting, which they were motivated to share with believers and nonbelievers alike. This was love in action.

Many of the early converts to "The Way" were from Judaism, where persons had long saved brownie stamps to earn salvation. The stamp books and the motivation of the Adapted Child were discarded for a more fulfilling life. Heaven was not some far off place in the musty future but a present experience. Here and now were the watchwords for Godliness. Though some persons expected the Lord to return to earth and set up some kind of an earthly kingdom, most of the people seemed content to live from day to day basking in the sunlight of God's love and goodness.

One of the qualities that was present in the primitive church was "glossolalia" or "speaking in tongues." This was conceived as a gift of the Natural Child, which responded to the Holy Spirit by openness and expectancy, and was a sign that God was involved in the worship experience. Peculiar experiences, voices, and mannerisms came about to and through the person experiencing this ecstatic gift. A whole congregation came under the power of this gift at the pentecostal service in Jerusalem, as recorded in Acts 2. Believers saw that this was evidence that the messianic age had begun and that they were part of God's plan.

Nonbelievers wrote these experiences off as evidence of drunkenness, irresponsibility, and emotionalism. But those who were of "The Way" saw them as evidence that God was pouring his Spirit out on human flesh not only in accordance with the prophesy of the Old Covenant but as promised by the risen Lord. The New Covenant was not by rules and form (Parent to Adapted Child) but by experiences and feelings (the Natural Child).

Speaking in tongues was a basic and necessary part of the New Testament church, occurring both in private and public worship. Not every believer had the ability to respond to the Holy Spirit in this unique way. Even those who could not turn on to God in this way were inspired and affected by those who had this ability and could share the insights and benefits of this ecstasy. All the believers seem to benefit by this gift of God.

Early leaders in the church felt compelled to justify this quality of worship. Peter, in his first sermon after the pentecostal experience, confronted the critics who ridiculed the gift of glossolalia, said it was hardly the effect of alcohol, since it was "only the third hour" and certainly not the result of a "happy hour" barroom experience. He cited the prophecy of Joel 2:28–32 and Psalm 16:8–11 as being fulfilled in the experience.

Speaking in tongues was not without abuses in the New Testament church. The early leaders felt that, uncontrolled, it could produce chaos and confusion. As noted in 1 Corinthians 14, Paul met these weaknesses by giving strong direction as to how the Adult dimension must supervise even the gift of glossolalia. He recognized that the ability to speak in tongues was a gift of the Holy Spirit. He did not forbid it since he actually shared the gift himself. He encouraged its use in private devotions, witnessing to nonbelievers, and in public worship, but with certain Adult restrictions: (1) Though it had value he recommended that the Adult would speak five words rather than ten thousand words spoken by the unsupervised Natural Child (14:19); (2) that public worship should be orderly (14:13–19); (3) that public worship be for edification (14:26); (4) that only two or three speak at a given worship service (14:27); (5) that there be someone to interpret (14:27); (6) and that all persons be involved in "weighing" or interpreting what is meant by the tongue. He makes the classic statement, "For God is not a God of confusion but of peace (1 Cor. 14:33)." He stresses the need for the Adult to be in control at a worship service. It is appropriate to "free the Child" but only under Adult supervision, lest there be confusion, distraction, and chaos. Some of the early worship services degenerated into noisy uproars of emotionalism where the Natural Child was in full control. Those in leadership soon insisted that Adult restrictions be applied whenever glossolalia became a part of worship.

An interesting account in the fifth chapter of Acts brings out the fact that not all the early believers were persuaded to give everything to the Lord. Some were still controlled by the Adapted Child who is reluctant to go all the way. Ananias and his wife, Sapphira, sold a piece of property and held back some of the proceeds. Bringing only a part of the cash to the sale they laid the money "at the apostles' feet." Evidently Peter knew that they were holding back, not only of their property, but also of their devotion and said, "Why has Satan filled your heart to lie to the Holy Spirit and to keep back part of the proceeds of the land? You have not lied to men but to God." Ananias felt so guilty ("NOT OK") that he probably had a coronary occlusion that resulted in his death. Three hours later, when she heard what had happened to her husband, and suffering from the same "NOT OK" feeling, Sapphira also had a heart attack and dropped dead on the spot. Both were buried as object lessons by the church as to what happens when a person "resists and lies" to the Holy Spirit, as well as the lesson of half-hearted service to God.

Stephen, the first martyr of the faith, had a promising future. In the dimension of the Natural Child under the supervision of the Adult he had performed and witnessed great signs and wonders of the kingdom of God. When he was formally charged with blasphemy, he gave a beautiful and historic witness to the faith of those who were appointed judge and jury to try his orthodoxy. Several features of his defense show not only that the Adult was in control but that his Natural Child was liberated. He had a face "like the face of an angel (Acts 6:15)," which is a nonverbal of the Natural Child. When he was later judged to be guilty of profaning Judaism his accusers became enraged (Parent). Stephen was "full of the Holy Spirit" (Natural Child) and even at his death he knelt down and said, "Lord Jesus, receive my spirit." What a simple, beautiful, and natural representation of the "OK Child." What an inspiration to all who heard of his faith and life. One of the men present at his martyrdom was Saul, who was later to become Paul, the apostle to the Gentiles. Just as Jesus had gone to his death in the dimension of the Natural Child under the supervision of the Adult, so had Stephen. And at least one man's life had been seriously affected by his childlike trust and faith. This man (Saul) became the champion of the Adult-controlled church, in conflict with those who would make "The Way" a sect of Judaism, requiring that a Christian convert come under the same legalism and traditionalism as a Jew.

On the Damascus road, Saul was converted to the faith. He had a religious experience in the dimension of the Natural Child. Feeling that he was doing God and man a service, Saul had been on his way to Damascus to persecute those claiming to be followers of "The Way." The physical qualities of his experience were "light," "a voice," "a vision," "a blindness," and then the recovery of his sight and new insight. He gave allegiance to the One who was formerly his enemy. His acceptance of "The Way" was not by reason and logic, nor was it by orthodoxy or conservatism. It was the response of the Natural Child of Saul to the Natural Child of God, the Holy Spirit. His whole personality, including his name, was changed from this experience. His Natural Child responded to the love and power of the Holy Spirit. He could never explain the experience at later times, but only to say, "I was once blind, but now I can see." It is through the senses of the Natural Child that a person can respond to the love of God. It has to be felt, not directed (Parent-Adapted Child) nor rationally accepted (Adult). This was the experience and witness of the first-century Christians.

Some leaders in the church saw the Christian faith as a new movement within Judaism. Not that the new experiences were unimportant; but they thought they needed the discipline and formalism of the Old Testament law. Converts were passionately sought and trained. The "Spirit" and "feeling" approach were suspected and conceived to be incomplete. A new convert must, in addition to accepting Jesus as Lord and the Holy Spirit as companion, also submit to the Old Testament law. Men converts had to be circumsized in accordance with the law of Moses. Holy days had to be kept, traditions had to be restored. Being a Christian was all right during the weekdays, but the holy days, the sabbath, and religious laws had to be strictly followed. Worship the risen Lord on Sunday, but also worship the God of Abraham, Isaac, and Jacob on Jewish holy days. A great controversy arose in the New Testament church between the Traditionalists and those who were attempting to follow the spirit and will of Jesus as revealed through the Holy Spirit. It was a struggle between the Parent-Adapted Child and the Natural Child supervised by the Adult. To muddy the waters, some persons had profaned themselves and the faith when they had put the Natural Child in control at the expense of the Adult who was trussed up in the closet. In the struggle some were able to liberate the Natural Child under the supervision of the Adult, while others got hung up on traditionalism and orthodoxy.

It was not long after the establishment of the church that there emerged the need for some sort of ecclesiastical control. The apostles had been hungry for some kind of precedence in the approaching kingdom of God and had even asked for special offices and powers when Jesus was in the physical dimension. These apostles wanted to be chief of staff or executive officer in the chain of command, to have request chits submitted through them for their approval before going to the commanding officer. The original disciples not only had asked for this privilege but had representatives and spokesmen plead for this authority.

Jesus condemned the motivation of the disciples as inappropriate and unnecessary. The greatest in the kingdom of heaven was really the servant of all. The original disciples had misunderstood what Jesus had said about this matter while he was in a physical body. After his death and resurrection the subject came up again. This time certain persons assumed authority, claiming "ordination" and claiming that special relationships automatically gave precedence and authority. Certain persons were anxious about position and power. A certain channel was established to safeguard the direction of the Holy Spirit and other graces of God. Soon, however, men in their humanness would become less concerned about their ministry and more about their authority, and thus begin to channel and dispense the grace of God. But whatever their motivation, the end result would be a limitation of the Holy Spirit. If the grace of God could be controlled by the whims and laws of men, the end result would either be legalism or favoritism, or the benefit would be determined to be nonessential or undesirable. For when people are low on experience, they become high on formalism, doctrine, and ritualism, which are the safeguards of orthodoxy.

The missionary journeys of the professionals came about at the promptings of the Holy Spirit. Neither the Parent nor the Adult could motivate the man, Paul, to leave the security of home and traditionalism to go to the undeserving and unloved. But Paul, under great hardships, ministered to these people. Not only were converts won to the faith, but the strength and dedication of Paul were solidified. Throughout his life he suffered from many of the hang-ups of modern men (sexuality, freedom, logic, orthodoxy), but Paul came through in an admirable way. His struggles were not ignored. They have become inspirational materials for persons in every century, urging discontent with formalism and orthodoxy and a return to the fundamental of belief, which is a relationship with God as revealed through the Son or the Holy Spirit.

One of the beautiful figures used by Paul which is consistent with the analysis and spirit of Jesus is the challenge of athletics, appealing to the Natural Child. The performance of the Christian faith can be aptly suggested by the athletic contests of the first century. Using the symbols of the olympics, Paul talked about the confrontations and struggles that the athlete faces in scrimmage and that a Christian faces in the game of life.

Jesus had said:

> But to what shall I compare this generation? It is like children sitting
> in the market places and calling to their playmates,
> "We piped to you, and you did not dance;
> we wailed, and you did not mourn."
>
> —Matthew 11:16–17

The description of "children in the market place" having their games and relationships invoked a response of either "to play" or "not to play." The challenge was there. The opportunity was there. The resources were there. The invitation was there. Only some ignored the opportunity, some rejected the offer, some were offended at the method. But the appeal was there. It was not accepted by the Adult (playing is unproductive), the Parent (playing is a waste of time), or the Adapted Child (playing does not bring brownie stamps). But to the Natural Child, playing is not only important but fun and fulfilling.

Paul made a beautiful analysis of the living of the Christian life and the confrontation that took place on the athletic field as a really important description of the Christian life which appealed not to the Parent, Adult, or Adaptive Child, but to the Natural or "OK Child."

The Christian faith is not a spectator sport. It is a contest that must be entered into and trained for, and effort made in, and victory pressed for and found. The image of a football fan in front of the TV screen, half smashed from overindulgence in beer, watching a confrontation on the playing field is not unlike some Christians approaching their faith. Religion for them is "choosing" a team, becoming a fan, and sticking with a club as long as it is having winning seasons. But when there are changes to be made, reorganization in the coaching staff, trading of players, some losing games, then the fans shift to a more "promising" team or else give up the sport altogether. Religion becomes a "half-smashed" expedient, to be closely followed when the home team is winning but to be forsaken when the going gets tough. Religion is also seen as a spectacle to be observed and criticized but with no responsibility for the decisions determined, the yards gained, or the errors made. The "sportsman" in front of the TV is like a churchman who observes an occasional happening in the church, from the dimension of either the Parent who is critical of the commercials, cheerleading, halftime show, and confrontation; or the Adapted Child who is looking for new ways of earning brownie stamps. Even the dimension of the Adult (who is a better coach or quarterback than the persons calling the plays and providing the strategy) is inadequate to feel the joy of the game as experienced on the playing field. The real nitty-gritty of the game of football is like the nitty-gritty of life. It has to be lived and experienced, not observed.

Paul has some interesting comments and views to share regarding the Christian experience. He states that it is like an athletic contest. Not only is there scrimmage but also preparation. He talks about the discipline (Adult) of training and competition. He states that an entrant into a track meet has to spend long hours of discipline and training. He must observe control in diet and structuring of time so that muscles and attitude be prepared. An athlete cannot compete favorably on the track or field unless his body and mind are under control. What goes into a person's makeup has an effect on what he does and also on what he accomplishes. If it is important that his muscles have stamina then it is also important that his mind expect the victory. And so he trains. He runs, he develops breath control, he builds stamina, he gets perseverance, he becomes mentally and physically motivated for the contest ahead.

Listen to Paul as he challenges the Natural Child.

Do you not know that in a race all the runners compete, but only one receives the prize? So run that you may obtain it. Every athlete exercises self-control in all things. They do it to receive a perishable wreath [a trophy], but we an imperishable.

—1 Corinthians 9:24–25

You were running well; who hindered you from obeying the truth?

—Galatians 5:7

Brethren, I do not consider that I have made it my own; but one thing I do, forgetting what lies behind and straining forward to what lies ahead, I press on toward the goal for the prize of the upward call of God in Christ Jesus. Let those of us who are mature [Controlled by the Adult] be thus minded; . . . only let us hold true to what we have attained.

—Philippians 3:13–16

Therefore, since we are surrounded by so great a cloud of witnesses, let us also lay aside every weight, and sin which clings so closely, and let us run with perseverance the race that is set before us, looking to Jesus the pioneer and perfecter of our faith, who for the joy that was set before him, endured the cross.

—Hebrews 12:1–2

Paul also used the image from the boxing arena which is more dramatic and bloody than the track meet. He states:

I do not run aimlessly, I do not box as one beating the air [shadow boxing]; but I pommel my body and subdue [discipline] it, lest after preaching to others I myself should be disqualified.

—1 Corinthians 9:26–27

I have fought the good fight, I have finished the race, I have kept the faith. Henceforth there is laid up for me the crown of righteousness, which the Lord, the righteous judge [the unprejudiced official], will award to me on that Day, and not only to me but also to all who have loved his appearing [the Natural Child].

—2 Timothy 4:7–8

This beautiful and significant description of the Christian life by Paul, whose name was changed from Saul, should give persons hope as to what can happen to a person who, like Paul, puts the pieces of the jigsaw puzzle of life together; but what can give meaning and fulfillment to life is available to all who through the Natural or OK Child can accept and receive the goodness of God. Life is like an athletic contest where persons are concerned about running a race and competing for a trophy. This trophy is not *earned* by the Adapted Child who saves sufficient brownie stamps but by the Natural Child who gleefully runs the race.

The Christian life is an athletic contest, not to be observed, but to be experienced. It is not a spectator sport to be observed on a boob tube some distance from the confrontation. But it is getting involved in the scrimmage; not certain of the victory, but certain only that the one who means most to you is involved in the struggle and that your leader and your goals are involved in the contest. Jesus is the quarterback who is the son of the owner of the team. He is involved in the confrontation and in the victory or defeat. He shares both with his teammates. He is the quarterback who is the son of the owner of the team who also shares the results of the confrontation. The reputation of the team stands or falls on its ability to meet the skirmishes of life and remain victorious. This is the kind of a leader Jesus is. This is the kind of a fellowship or team he commands. Permission to carry the ball is not given on the basis of favoritism but to those who can make yardage, enjoy playing the game, and bring victory to the home team.

Paul, reflecting on the uncertainty between victory and defeat, said we are fools for Christ's sake. Only those who have known the feeling of confrontation and struggle can possibly know the joy and sweetness of victory and the trophy which symbolizes it.

Joy is the trademark of the Christian. When a person knows joy, he is a member in good standing. When a person does not know it or tries to counterfeit it, he is a phony and a fake!

The difference between Old Testament and New Testament joy is that there is joy in tribulation in the New Testament. When all things are on "Go" and everything is wonderful it is easy to be a believer. But the New Covenant joy is built upon a relationship that sees joy not only in victory over evil but in God's involvement in the struggle. The Old Covenant had singing, shouting, noise, uproar, loud voices; using various instruments like the harp, cymbals, trumpet, flute, stringed instruments; dancing, clapping, sacrificing, celebrating harvest; enjoying personal triumph, prosperity, recovery of health, etc. as means for rejoicing in God. But the New Covenant sees thanksgiving and joy in the fact that God is with us in the struggle, and that with him we will be victorious. Thanks be to God who gives the victory.

The mark of joy is a Christian mark. Jesus promised and gives joy to those who respond to his spirit and feeling. The potential for joy is present as much in this century as in the first century among those who respond to his love. It is the Natural Child liberated by the Adult who is both ready and willing to respond to the love of God as revealed in Jesus and the Holy Spirit.

The early Christians had a positive approach to religion and life. They were not hung up on sin or "NOT OK-ness." Not that evil was ignored or soft-pedaled; the New Testament Christian had an "I'M OK—YOU'RE OK" outlook toward life. Like the shepherds on the hillside, they expected angels to sing and wonderful things to happen. Like the wise men from the east who followed a star, the early

Christians were not hung-up on sophisticated proof and analysis. Like Mary and Joseph, the Christians humbly expected God to share life with them and use their bodies and resources to share his love with the world. "Joy to the world" was the feeling and motivation of the church of the first century.

The Lord's Supper was not just a somber observance of the passion and death of Jesus but an affirmation of his resurrection as well. Rather than seeing in the Lord's Supper a sorrowful death, the thrill of eternal life and happiness was stressed. The Lord's Supper was like a little person giving a tea party and inviting his friends to come to the party in the dimension of the Natural Child. It was a time of celebration and victory. The bread and wine of the eucharist were received, not unlike the cookies and juice of the Natural Child's tea party.

It was Jesus who commemorated the fellowship around the table, and directed that his believers periodically share in the fellowship meal using the symbols of the bread and wine. Without the supervision of the Adult, though, even the eucharist became abused and the symbolism lost. The Natural Child became more interested in eating and drinking than in remembering the purpose of the sacrament and the spirit of the one being honored. It was necessary for Paul to put some Adult controls on the sacrament in order that the memorial meal not be desecrated and that the people not fail to derive spiritual benefit from the observance.

Paul records the first written record of the institution and observance of the Lord's Supper:

> For I received from the Lord what I also delivered to you, that the Lord Jesus on the night when he was betrayed took bread, and when he had given thanks, he broke it, and said, "This is my body which is for you. Do this in remembrance of me." In the same way also the cup, after supper, saying, "This cup is the new covenant in my blood. Do this, as often as you drink it, in remembrance of me." For as often as you eat this bread and drink the cup, you proclaim the Lord's death until he comes.
>
> Whoever, therefore, eats the bread or drinks the cup of the Lord in an unworthy manner will be guilty of profaning the body and blood of the Lord. Let a man examine himself, and so eat of the bread and drink of the cup. For any one who eats and drinks without discerning the body eats and drinks judgment upon himself. That is why many of you are weak and ill, and some have died.
>
> —1 Corinthians 11:23–30

In this passage Paul reminds the people of the sacred meaning of Holy Communion and how to eliminate abuses in its celebration. Self-examination is important. Temperance is a watchword. The Adult supervision of the Natural Child must be present or else the eucharist will be profaned and the significance and spiritual grace lost. If these words of Paul become a way of supervising the Natural Child, then the direction is helpful. But for many in the church today the words of Paul become so authoritarian that the Natural Child never gets to enjoy the sacrament, thus losing the real benefit of the meal. They become like the salt without taste that Jesus had spoken about earlier. "You are the salt of the earth; but if salt has lost its taste, how shall its saltness be restored? It is no longer good for anything except to be thrown out and trodden under foot by men (Matt. 5:13)."

Salt is a very useful substance and Jesus complimented his followers by calling them "the salt of the earth." Salt is useful as a seasoning, preservative, purifying agent and even a means of lowering the freezing point of water. But if salt loses its flavor it is good for nothing.

A Christian who cannot activate the Natural Child is like salt without taste. These persons may look like the real thing, talk like the real thing, act like the real thing, but they are only role-playing. Their faith is a veneer, their religion a sham. Their righteousness is a pretense. Their dedication is only an imitation.

The believers of the first century were in the dimension of the Natural Child. They had seasoning and flavor in life. Life was to be tasted and enjoyed. They were literally "the salt of the earth," adding zest and significance to life. They did not lose their saltiness but they did get hung up when the Adult failed to supervise the Natural Child. They had a quality of life and a zest for loving that Christians of the twentieth century would do well to seek and enjoy. But they serve also as a reminder of what can happen, even in the church, when the Adult does not supervise the Natural Child. Life can become just hedonistic (pleasure-seeking) unless the Adult gives direction and supervision.

It may be that the first-century Christians were sometimes void of not only the Parent hang-ups of the law and orthodoxy, but also the disciplining feature of reason of the Adult; but they had a quality and purpose of living which is not only admirable for those of this century but also desirable for today. We have organized religion of many facets from the freewheeling emotionalism of the "Holy Rollers" to the discipline and doctrine of the Fundamentalists and Traditionalists in all denominations. The quality of life that is missing today is love in action which expects God to be present in human relationships. The necessary now is important. "Pie in the sky, by and by" may be worth waiting for, but to have a right relationship with God and man in the now and present is well worth having. The believers of the first century may have been lacking in their explanation of systematic theology, but they had a meaningful relationship with God and each other.

It is not difficult to get a dollar donation today or get a church wife to bake a pie or cook a chicken for a bazaar or church supper. But the most important dimension lacking in the church of the twentieth century is the fact that God lives and dwells in us and that our lives are not only in his care but that he shares our joys and disappointments with us. This is God in life. This is God relating with men. This is God sharing life with men. This is the faith and approach of the New Testament church. This is the motivation that causes a person to "shoot the works," to "bet it all," "to go all the way." It cannot be rationally proven but it is not irrational either, for the overtones give health and happiness. It is a quality of life and living that Jesus talked about and lived. It parallels the finding of a pearl of great price or the happiness and joy that comes when something that was lost is now found. It is the quality of life that Jesus illustrated in parable form. It is the kingdom of God in this life that can be sensuously enjoyed here and now by those who can free the Child and keep it under Adult supervision.

Paul talked about being a "fool for Christ's sake" as a dimension of the Natural Child. Reason and logic can lead to a certain point. Reason and logic are of great benefit. But there comes the time when the person must make the "leap of faith," "shoot the works," "launch out into the unknown." When he does he experiences some of the goodness and blessings that Jesus tried to make possible for men. If this would be possible through law, Moses would have been able to incorporate it in legalism. If it would have been possible through reason, the Greek and Roman scholars and students would have given us great insights. But it comes only through the response of the Natural Child who approaches life through wonder, openness, spontaneity, enthusiasm, joy, responsiveness, sensuousness, experience, faith. Through these avenues can the Natural Child find expression and meaning in life and the joy of life. This is what Jesus taught and lived. And it is true for this and other centuries of life.

The early Christians put all material resources into a common pot, all living was shared, all grace was experienced: the kingdom of heaven was among them to be accepted and enjoyed in this life and in the life to come. The goodness of God was here and now, in this life and in the life to come. Grace was conceived as a gift to be accepted and enjoyed, love was a reality and the Holy Spirit of God was the sign and seal of the love of God.

The early church of New Testament times was built upon an experience. It was a confrontation of God with men. The important part of this relationship was man's response to God's love. It was not to be observed, measured, tested, obeyed or served, only to be accepted and enjoyed. This was the response of the Natural Child under the supervision of the Adult. Reason and logic are essentials in safeguarding the faith. But first there must be an experience and this experience must be centered in a loving personality. This truth sets men free today as it did in the first century.

The early believers had an experience with the personality and spirit of Jesus. It gave them a quality of life and a zest for living that they never had known before. In their excitement they quit their jobs, sold their property, put the proceeds into a common fund, began communal living, lived in daily expectancy that God would accomplish wonderful signs and miracles among them and anticipated the second coming of Christ to set up God's fulfilled kingdom on earth. Some were disappointed that the Parousia or the second coming of Christ was temporarily delayed. Some later grew disillusioned and depressed when the Natural Child expected certain things to happen and they did not happen in their lifetimes. But those who had the faith of the Natural Child undergirded by the logic and reasoning of the Adult caused them to make responsible decisions and set realistic goals. When the Adult makes choices based upon fact and data, a person can face the present and the future with confidence and the past without anxiety.

The liberation of the Natural Child was a reality for the early Christians but they learned the necessity for the Adult to supervise the qualities of the Natural Child. It was this motivation that inspired the New Testament Christians to face difficult and critical situations and still maintain a sense of joy and fulfillment. Some went to prison or death for living and believing "The Way," but they went cheerfully and gladly for they had the assurance that the Lord was with them. They knew joy in persecution, joy in imprisonment, joy in poverty, joy in the loss of property, joy in standing fiery trials, joy in torture, joy in suffering and in death. The promise of Jesus was, "These things I have spoken to you, that my joy may be in you, and that your joy may be full (John 15:11)." The joy of Jesus was a reality to the early Christians and their cups were running over.

PART **III**

*Application
of Transactional
Analysis
in the Church, Home,
and Community*

7

The Three Dimensions
of Deity

Transactional Analysis is a helpful device to understand the motivations and makeup of people. It teaches the trinity of personality, that a person in every situation comes through in one of the three dimensions, as Parent, as Adult, as Child. This is not three different people nor is it role-playing. It is the real person in each dimension even though the shades of personality are quite different. When a person is in the Adult dimension he is no more or less a person than he is when the Child or Parent is exposed. Each dimension is a useful part of the personality. What makes a certain dimension good or bad is whether it is appropriate. The technique of Transactional Analysis helps us isolate the facets of personality, particularly as we interact with others. To be able to evaluate which dimension is in control, especially as we evaluate the other person, produces great insights and understanding. It is known that when a person feels strongly about something he will probably show great emotion. When the facts are important, on the other hand, then a genuine effort will be made to share these data with others. The important point is that whether emotions are being shown or whether data is being shared, to be able to ascertain the dimension that is in control will help to understand the "message" that is being communicated. To communicate effectively one must be able to understand the persons involved in the communication, both the sender and the receiver. The message is important, but insights about the person sending and receiving the message not only make the communication clearer but draw the sender and the receiver closer together in the process.

A father is no more or less real as he interacts with his children as Parent, Adult, or Child. Whether the dimension in control is appropriate is what makes the relationship helpful or hurtful. In life and injury situations it is helpful for a father to come through emotionally in an authoritarian and demanding way (Parent). In other situations he shows other emotions, as he exposes his feelings in openness, spontaneity, wonder, enthusiasm, self-abandonment, sensuousness, unselfishness, and love (Natural Child). But these two facets of his personality must be under the supervision of reason (Adult) or else his demands will be dictatorial and his actions unpredictable. Without the supervision of the Adult there would be confusion, anxiety, and fear in the children as they attempt to relate to their senior. It would be helpful for the children to be able to identify these dimensions of the father as they share life with him. In the same way the father would find it helpful to evaluate the children as they interact in the same dimensions.

Theologians of every age have labored to explain the personality of God. They recognize that the revelation of God varies from that of authoritarian figure to that of loving companion. But God is predictable, not only in being limited by dependable universal laws but also in that his love is dependable, because wisdom and reason undergird both! To describe the mystery of this revelation, theologians formulated the doctrine of the Trinity, God's revelation in three shades of his personality: Father (Parent), Son (Adult), and Holy Spirit (Natural Child). This is not three different "gods" but three manifestations of his personality, three dimensions of his being. God may well have other dimensions in his personality but these three have been experienced in ancient and modern times by sensitive and discerning persons.

It is believed that since man is made in the image of God, both man and God bear family characteristics and personality. We have seen that Jesus reflected life in three dimensions (Parent, Adult, and Child). In his humanity he reflected the authoritarian (Parent), reason (Adult), and love (Natural Child). He was "son" of Mary and Joseph, grew up in a traditional Jewish home; experienced the love of mother, father, brothers, sisters, and friends; was trained not only in the traditional Jewish approach to God and man through obedience to legalistic expectations and demands but also in a practical theology that life was basically a loving response to the love of God. Religion was a series not of "thou shalts" and "thou shalt nots" but natural opportunities to know God and man by the intellect and respond to God and man through the senses. The historical Jesus had a beautiful potential for relating to God and man that all persons possess. His mission was to share this truth with those who would respond to his teaching and living. He gave his life in loving sacrifice to give mankind both the medium and the opportunity to enter the kingdom of heaven and share the kingdom of heaven with others. The grace of God is not something to be earned by diligent effort but to be accepted as a gift. The cross became the symbol of God's love being shared with humanity but also became God's power to break the "death" barrier which had long separated the divine and human. In a special way God used Jesus to reveal his true personality and nature.

History is a record of God endeavoring to communicate his personality to mankind. His Parent dimension had long been known by the world in the legalistic approach to obedience. The Old Testament record speaks of God as "Creator," "Law Giver," "Judge," "Military Leader," "King," "Owner." God's personality was seen as belonging to a mighty, powerful, omnipotent, judgmental, jealous, righteous, indig- nant Being who, in perfection, demanded perfection in his followers. He was seen as "OK" by his people who were "NOT OK." The people, hung up in the Adapted Child dimension, could only see God in one dimension: Parent. Even though God endeavored to share his total nature with the people, the Adapted Child of the people was only able to know God in the Parent dimension. It was when Jesus responded to the love of God that the other dimension of God's personality was known by men. It took not only his life and teaching but the cross and empty tomb to continue to show the revelation of God's personality. The potential to know God in three dimensions was always present in the world but it was through Jesus that people seemed to "understand" and respond to God's true nature and love.

There were individuals living before Jesus who had caught glimpses of God's personality in other than the Parent dimension. But their response to and their sharing of these insights seemed to have little effect upon men who would not give up their Adapted Child dimension. The cross and the empty tomb are historic realities that vividly focus the true nature of God and bring about the appropriate response of man; they became the necessary tools and communication symbols to reunite God with man and man with God; salvation is complete.

God is just, righteous and mighty. He is Creator, Lawgiver and

Omnipotent. He is King, Leader, and Father. He is Heavenly Parent. Some Old Testament personages had glimpses of God as Heavenly Parent. Some of the references are as follows:

Do you thus requite the Lord,
    you foolish and senseless people?
Is not he your father, who created you,
    who made you and established you?

—Deuteronomy 32:6

Father of the fatherless and protector of widows
    is God in his holy habitation.

—Psalm 68:5

Yet, O Lord, thou art our Father;
    we are the clay, and thou art our potter;
    we are all the work of thy hand.

—Isaiah 64:8

Have we not all one father? Has not one God created us?
Why then are we faithless to one another, profaning the
    covenant of our fathers?

—Malachi 2:10

As a father pities his children,
    so the Lord pities those who fear him.
For he knows our frame;
    he remembers that we are dust.

—Psalm 103:13–14

There is some value in seeing God as Divine Parent. This is an important and meaningful insight into the nature and personality of God. Some sensitive souls living before the birth of Jesus were able to experience this dimension of God. God was seen as the progenitor of the human race, who had designed and shaped man out of the dust. Though these people were close to the truth about God as Parent their conception of God was through the Adapted Child of the people, indebted to the Parent who had given them existence. Fear, obedience, and dependence were considered to be the appropriate responses to these insights about God. In the presence of God the people felt "NOT OK."

It was Jesus who taught man to view the Divine Parent through the dimension of the "OK" or Natural Child. In a very real and special way Jesus referred to God as being "my heavenly Father." It was a special relationship that was available also to others who could approach God as heavenly Father through the dimension of the "OK" or Natural Child. He taught people to pray, "Our Father who art in heaven . . . ," to trust, love, honor, serve, and know God in the dimension of the Divine Parent who was desirous of an intimate relationship with his children. The Divine Parent is motivated by love, but his love is seasoned with rules and logic. As with any earthly father worthy of the name, God's parental dimension is guided by responsibility. He is lawgiver, but his laws safeguard the rights of his children. He is judge, but his judgment is seasoned with justice and love. He is creator, but his creation is done through dependable natural laws. He is omnipotent, but his power is channeled through an orderly universe. He is Parent, but his fatherhood is reflected in a loving relationship with his children.

There are times when the stern Divine Parent demands obedience of the Adapted Child. About life and death situations he tells his children what to seek and what to avoid. There is no such thing as committing a little adultery or a little blasphemy or a little bit of murder. Disobedience in these areas, however slight, causes a break in the relationship with the Divine Parent. It is not on the part of the Parent but on the part of the Adapted Child. The Natural Child avoids these pitfalls for his motivation—a loving response to God's love as practiced in human relationships—would have no reason to harm his fellowman in any of these areas. He respects not only the rights and property of others but also the human worth and dignity of all members of God's family.

One of the three dimensions of God as seen by mankind then is that of Divine Parent. This area of the personality of God helps man not only relate to the Source and Power of his life but also to fellow humans. If God is Divine Parent then members of the family of God are seen as brothers and sisters equally entitled to the family name and legacy. Many persons have conceived of God as some sort of a divine parent; but it was Jesus who taught and lived the theology that God is a *loving* Divine Parent who craves an intimate and loving relationship with his children.

It was Jesus who also helps us understand the second dimension of the triune nature of God: that of Wisdom or Word which can also be called the Divine Adult. Remember that the purpose of the Adult dimension is to assemble and evaluate truth, make logical decisions and then stick to the decisions; the Adult dimension also evaluates the inputs of the Parent dimension, controlling it when it is inappropriate, but liberating the Natural Child and then supervising his activities. The Adult dimension keeps the dimensions of personality appropriate, constantly evaluating relationships and facts.

The Divine Adult is that part of the nature of God that keeps his personality appropriate and dependable. It is the key to the character of God, making responsible decisions then assuming responsibility for the consequences of those decisions.

The Divine Adult was in control in the creation of life. The New Testament uses the word "Logos" translated "The Word" to describe this facet in the personality of God.

> In the beginning was the Word, and the Word was with God, and the Word was God. He was in the beginning with God; all things were made through him, and without him was not anything made that was made. In him was life, and the life was the light of men. The light shines in the darkness, and the darkness has not overcome it.
>
> —John 1:1–5

The universe was not made haphazardly or without planning; it was made out of heavenly reason and data. The universe was made by a responsible God who was controlled by logic, dependability, wisdom, and love. God chose to make the world; he was willing to assume responsibility for this choice. The Divine Adult was in control. The creation story in Genesis states that when God made man he assumed responsibility for his creation. Since the Divine Adult was in control, God was able to live with the products of his creation. Only one time did the Divine Adult lose control: that was in the destruction of human life except for Noah and his family. Since that time God has been able to live with the product of his creation because the Divine Adult was in control.

In a very special way Jesus teaches us of the wisdom and responsibility of the personality of God. "And the Word became flesh and dwelt among us, full of grace and truth; we have beheld his glory, glory as of the only Son from the Father (John 1:14)." The Word became flesh, it became human form. Not only was there the intellectual Word, the spoken Word, the living Word, but now the Word became human flesh and blood. The Divine Adult was in human form. God's Wisdom dwelt with men in a very special way in the life and person of Jesus.

When Jesus lived in the first century he was the fruit of Mary's body. He bore the resemblance to the human family. But he also, in his personality, was the Divine Adult in human form. The divine truth of God was incarnated in human flesh. The eternal wisdom of God now shared life with humanity. But Jesus was seen not as "super person," or "superstar" as some in our day would describe him. He was a man among men in whom a dimension of God chose to dwell. The people of the first century were impressed by him, but not until after his death and resurrection did they attribute to him the nature of the Divine Adult. He was simply referred to as the Teacher, Master, Friend, Lord, the Nazarene, the carpenter, the son of Mary. It was not until after the resurrection that both the name Jesus and the title Christ were combined. Jesus was then set apart by God. God's nature dwelled in him in a very special way. After the resurrection people saw him as the Incarnate Word of God, the personification of God's Truth, God's Son. But during his lifetime, when he lived and dwelled with men, his humanness was the most evident feature of his personality. God was in Jesus; but God is also incarnate in every person who is responsive to his Truth; who is willing to put blood and flesh, muscle and bone into permitting the love and truth of God to live in him and control his personality.

Obviously Jesus of Nazareth was not involved in the creation process at the beginning of time. But the spirit of truth, the Divine Adult, the Eternal Word who was the means and the method of creation was a part of the personality of Jesus. After his death and resurrection this facet of God's personality was discerned to have been present in human form and dwelt with men. This was not the first time that the *truth* of God was personified in the flesh, for the concept in a lesser way is also found in the Old Testament in Job, Proverbs, and the Wisdom of Solomon. The truth can also dwell among and with men of every century.

The third dimension of the Trinity, the Holy Spirit, personifies the transcendence of God and his involvement with men. Another name for this dimension of God is the Divine Child. Just as the Father and the Son (the Divine Parent and the Divine Adult) are personally distinct from one another, so is the Holy Spirit, the Divine Child, a unique dimension of God. The three are separate dimensions of the same personality. They reinforce and augment one another; they proceed from one another; they honor one another; they complete and fulfill one another. One purpose flows through them all; one substance composes them all; one motivation guides them all. The overall personality of God is love. The Holy Spirit is the love of God shared with men. The ancient symbol for the Trinity is three interlaced circles. This figure has been used to show the threefold nature of the personality of God: God in three persons, or three manifestations of the divine godhead. The three circles are interlaced to show that the same power of love flows through all dimensions. This ancient symbol is found today in stained glass windows, altar paraments, and clergy vestments. The circles which are all the same size show the triune aspects of God as experienced by men. It has been a meaningful symbol in the church's life for centuries. Now that the personality of God is plumbed by the method of Transactional Analysis we see that the ancient three-circle design effectively symbolizes the three dimensions of the personality of God. Figure 8 shows the application of this truth using this modern technique.

The Divine Parent (Father) finds a response in either the Adapted or Natural Child of man. The Divine Adult (Son) deals with the Adult in man. The Divine Natural Child (Holy Spirit) confronts the Natural Child of man.

One of the great insights contained within the first thirty-nine books of the Bible (the Old Testament) is that which pictures man made in the image of God. The next twenty-seven books (the New Testament) picture God in the image of man (Jesus Christ). The total dimension of God and man is revealed through the person of the Holy Spirit. This completes the dimension of Deity and assures man that God is personal and dwells with men, sharing their lives, their hopes, their aspirations, their problems, their shortcomings, their weaknesses, and their joys.

God was not completely understood through the dimension of Parent. The law, with its discipline, demands, and ritual give us a snapshot of God in one dimension. Nor was God completely understood through the dimension of logic and reason called Adult. That there are laws, and that these laws are dependable and understandable, is a fact of life. That the mind can logically understand one facet of the personality of God is an important insight. But God is more than Law (Parent) and Reason (Adult). He is love in action (Natural Child).

The most important insight about communication (and God is in the communication business) is not what a person says or what he knows he has said or what he meant to say, but what the hearer or receiver has "heard." Sometimes the message gets garbled in the process of communication. It has been the experience of every person to have been misunderstood when he thought his message and logic were clear

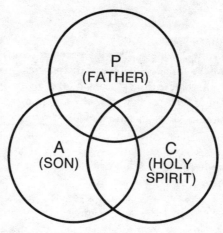

TRANSACTIONAL ANALYSIS SYMBOL FOR THE TRINITY

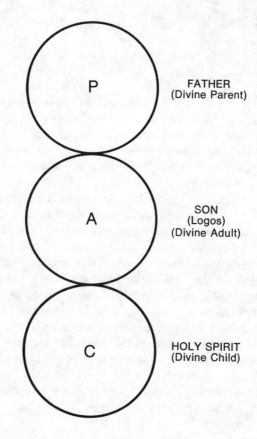

TRANSACTIONAL ANALYSIS SYMBOL FOR THE TRINITY

FIGURE 8

and open. Sometimes people hear only what they want to hear and expect to hear. But the message must get through; communication must take place. To determine what a person has heard requires the consideration of "feedback." Even God himself must use the technique of receiving "feedback" from those who would communicate with him, understand his personality and learn his nature.

The children of Israel evaluated the communication and personality of God as parent; he was law-giver, military leader, judge, and king. The persons who shared experiences with Jesus understood God as teacher, leader, philosopher, and lord. This dimension of God's personality was seen as Adult. Both of these groups gave "feedback" to God. The believers who knew the Holy Spirit, the counselor, the companion, the comforter, and the friend knew the great emotion of God with us. The Holy Spirit is the Natural Child of God that shares life with the Natural Child of men. It is the source of joy from God bringing about joy in the hearts of those who respond to God. Love is the dimension of the Natural Child in God or man. The response to love is in the dimension of the Natural Child, who is open, filled with wonder, enthusiastic, expectant, spontaneous, self-abandoned, optimistic, unprejudiced, and sensuous. Making love is the quality and purpose of the Natural Child.

Persons of every age have responded to the Natural Child of God in the dimension of the Natural Child of man. Meaningful and personal experiences of man and God have taken place since the beginning of time. It was not until after the resurrection and ascension of Jesus that the promise of sharing the Holy Spirit with men in a new and revealing way was fulfilled. On the day of Pentecost recorded in Acts 2, the third dimension of God was given to a group of responsive persons. For the first time a group of people assembled in the dimension of the Natural Child. They were overpowered and overwhelmed by the Natural Child of God which is the Holy Spirit. The spiritual ecstasy, the joy, the satisfaction and fulfillment of life came to these people as a group. Jesus had promised the Holy Spirit; the reality of the Holy Spirit had been known by individuals in the past. But for the first time a whole congregation experienced the beauty of God's revelation in the dimension of the Natural Child. A third portrait of God was captured on the film of human understanding. God was with men. God was involved in the business of living and loving. In a special way God was relating to men in the third dimension, the facet of the Natural Child.

The Christians of the first century were prepared for the confrontation of God with man in this dimension.

Now that the children of men and God felt "OK" they could respond to God in the "I'M OK—YOU'RE OK" position. This is the first time in the history of mankind that this relationship was possible. Jesus had done for man what man could not do for himself: he had made things right with God. Rightness or righteousness was now established through the second dimension of the Trinity. Now there could be openness and complete loving between God and man. The "OK Child" of man could respond to the "OK Child" of God. They could share life and living in a beautiful way that was not possible before. As Jesus gave us insights about God as Father (Parent) and God as Son (Adult), he now gives us the insights of God as Holy Spirit (Natural Child) and makes it possible for man to respond in the Natural Child dimension.

In the Old Testament there is seen a trinity of God and God's will: the law (Parent), wisdom (Adult), and prophecy (Natural Child). But it was when God chose to reveal to the world his Adult dimension in the person of Jesus that the third dimension became a special reality to men. Remember the point of communication is not what the communicator knows he wants to say, or has said, but what the hearer "hears." In the giving of the Holy Spirit, the Natural Child of God, man was able to "hear" and "feel" and "see" and "know" the true personality of God, which is love.

It was at the Council of Nicea in 325 that the doctrine of the Trinity was formulated, though the conception of God in three dimensions had been known by some discerning persons even in Old Testament periods. But the "snapshots" of God were given to the world in a new and meaningful way in the New Covenant period, when Jesus showed the data of God and the kingdom, insisting that God desired to be loved rather than obeyed. It was the giving of the Holy Spirit that completed the third dimension of God, that of God sharing life and emotions with men.

8

Which Dimension
Takes You to Church?

If the assumption of Transactional Analysis is correct—that in every situation, every transaction, every relationship, a person comes through in one of three dimensions—just which one is in control when a person goes to church/synagogue/temple? What is the motivation for going to church? How regularly does a person go? What does he expect to find when he goes? What does he expect to do when he makes this effort? What kind of prayers does he pray? How does he respond to the order and mechanics of worship? Does he participate in the ritual? Does he sing the hymns? Is he alert or does he frequently sleep during the service?

It is difficult and maybe a little dangerous to generalize about the motivations of people, especially in as threatening a situation as a person's religion. Like politics and sex, a person may have great emotions about the subject of religion, yet he may find it difficult to deal intelligently with the subject, for he may sometimes have more feelings than facts. It becomes threatening for many to tamper with feelings about God. These feelings are formulated at a very early age and are carefully protected throughout life. Sometimes people seem to be unwilling or unable to mature in their conception of God, so they perpetuate misconceptions and hang-ups learned in childhood. God is "pictured" as an old man with a long white beard and rosy cheeks, who carefully evaluates the minute details of a person's life, rewarding obedience with gifts and disobedience with displeasure and rejection. At the time when children are "taught" about Santa Claus they are also "taught" about God; for a small data computer (Adult) in a little person, there seems to be a great similarity between the two. Is it any wonder that children are sometimes unable to differentiate between what is fact and what is fancy, especially when the authority figures in their lives seem to know more about Santa Claus than they do about God? To confuse and mislead the children even more, it is on Christmas Day that both are honored as well as "appeased." The Christmas season also has "carols" and "secular tunes," "camels" and "reindeers," "a baby" and "doll babies," "angels" and "Santa's helpers," "church bells" and "sleigh bells," "kingly gifts" and "colored packages."

Christmas is an important holy day for the Christian; so is Easter. Again there is a counterbalance between the sacred and the secular. Peter, not the disciple but the Cottontail; new clothes, not grave clothes, chicks, bunnies, and ducklings, not the resurrected Christ; the Easter Bunny, not the Easter Christ; colored egg hunt, not the search for the resurrected Lord. It is believed that the secular has been substituted for the sacred because the sacred has lost its meaning and importance. What is needed is not a housecleaning of "make believe" but an honest evaluation of the facts of life (Adult), then liberation of the Natural Child under the supervision of the Adult.

It is the Adapted Child that "prepares" for Santa Claus, carefully earning sufficient brownie stamps by disciplined living to assure a good harvest of gifts. For many persons it is the same motivation as they approach their "god" in worship. The long months of visiting the toy shops (redemption centers) and studying gift catalogs prepare the Adapted Child so he can anticipate his "rewards." The Adapted Child is not "good for nothing," he is "good for something." The long months and years of diligent effort and "study" as well as the encouragement of the spokesmen who talk about it (preachers, Sunday school teachers, fathers, mothers) and reading the catalogs (Bible, prayer books, and church literature), prepare the Adapted Child to anticipate what "gifts" are available and how to assemble sufficient brownie stamps to secure valuable gifts at the redemption center.

I believe that the primary motivation for church attendance and religious devotion today is the Adapted Child who goes to church for the following reasons:

1. To please the Parent within and the authority figures without.

"It would be great to get both of them off of one's back, even just for a few minutes."

2. To hear what is being offered at the redemption center. "A little window shopping is really great fun."

3. To learn how to get brownie stamps for doing "good" and refraining from doing "bad." "Brownie stamp collecting is just about the most important hobby in the world."

4. To verify "goodness" by bringing the heavenly bookkeeping up to date. "Make certain heaven is aware of my diligence and their records agree with mine."

5. To be around others who are busy filling their own brownie stamp books. "Blest be the tie that binds."

6. To encourage each other to "shop" at the "right" places giving brownie stamps. "Some churches do not give the right color brownie stamps."

7. To support the institution that keeps the redemption center going. "I have a responsibility to the company."

8. To maintain the institution that sponsors the publicity and educational programs. "My presence and financial gifts are important."

9. To hear "Rah! Rah! Rah!" sermons for brownie stamp collecting. "A good commercial is great to stimulate dedication and obedience."

10. To learn singing commercials and jingles for brownie stamp collecting. "Catchy tunes and clever lyrics grab you when you shave and shine your shoes."

11. To learn new ways to get brownie stamps and the times and places where double and triple brownie stamps are offered. "Certain days of the week and certain transactions bring bonus stamps."

12. To take "graduate" courses in brownie stamp collecting. "When you do it for many years you must have bigger and more difficult programs."

13. To help everyone find a useful outlet for service in the program. "Everyone can be a cheerleader, song leader, musician, or scriptwriter for the brownie stamp program."

14. To formulate a class for teaching others about the importance and satisfaction of saving brownie stamps. "A children's class would be a fine opportunity but hopefully the age group would

not be such that the children would question the technique of stamp collecting."

15. To make everyone missionary minded, both home and foreign missions. Be certain to count the converts. "Sponsor branch offices so that people in other communities can learn about brownie stamps and have the benefits of stamp collecting."

16. To feel good and find a purpose in life and something you can do well. "Everyone can save brownie stamps and do it well."

17. To work diligently in the established program so that you will not have time to think about your own inadequacies and sins. "Keep from feeling guilty and 'NOT OK' by maintaining a busy schedule of helping others."

18. To get what is rightfully yours, what you justly deserve. "You have been working hard and long and have something wonderful coming to you."

19. To have the authority and concrete proof that goals are being reached and progress is underway. "There is something factual about counting your pages of brownie stamps."

20. To be obedient to the Lord's will. "After all, he said that one who does the will of the Lord will be rewarded."

The Adapted Child never is able completely to please the Parent within or the authority figures without. He feverishly tries to get these taskmasters off his back and have a moment of peace. He must rally some support, turning to others who are involved in brownie stamp collecting and to the "one" who supposedly invented the system. He approaches life, his fellowman, and his God through his "NOT OK" position. He knows he is "NOT OK." He likes feeling "NOT OK." Terms he uses to describe himself are "worm," "sinner," "unclean," "unrighteous," "sinful," "evil," "unworthy," "tainted," and "polluted."

He sees others as "NOT OK," but there are degrees of being "NOT OK." He knows how many brownie stamps he has collected as well as how many he deserves. He also is quick to point out the comparison between the thickness of his brownie stamp book compared to others who do not save stamps. From his "NOT OK" position he sees others who do not save stamps as even less deserving than he, but feels that someday he will have it over them. He has more "assets" than the noncollector. He has authority on his side. He is a company man. He must faithfully make an effort to prove his devotion and to prove that he takes his religion seriously. Since he is "NOT OK," he must work hard to become "OK," to "earn" the accolades of his companions and the congratulations of heaven.

Much good in the community and the world comes about through the efforts of the Adapted Child working "to beat hell" in his own life and in the lives of others. People who have an organized approach to life, who have established not only goals but ethical rules and procedures, can be nice people to have living next door. People who follow a legalistic approach to life and religion do offer the home and community a stability which is desirable. The only drawback is that it is not Christian; that it is not taught or practiced by Jesus Christ.

In some churches legalism dominates reason. God's will is plain. It is incorporated in laws. Some "Christians" believe that obedience to the "spiritual" laws is proof of discipleship and assures one of eternal salvation. Living a Christian life pleases God by doing the "good" and refraining from the "bad." When the ten commandments fail to give direction other regulations are established. The end justifies the means, and the means are clearly established in "shalts" and "shalt nots."

A good illustration of a law that is formulated even when the New Testament teaching fails to legislate is dancing. The Fundamentalist states that dancing is a sin. There is no basis for this position either in the Old or New Testament. But these persons state that a Christian does not dance. The rationale is that dancing causes persons to be sensuously oriented and that contact through dancing may produce disastrous results. So they say dancing is a sin and must be avoided and denied. "Thou shalt not dance," becomes a commandment on equal par with "Thou shalt not commit adultery," for dancing is seen as the first step to adultery. If you dance you are not a Christian. If you refrain from dancing for religious reasons you are a Christian. Each time you meet the temptation to dance with a "no" you receive a brownie stamp to be pasted in your brownie stamp book. Each time you tell another that "dancing is a sin," or, even better, that you do not dance because you are a Christian, you get a brownie stamp to paste in your book. And when you see someone who claims to be a Christian participating in dancing, you condemn him to hell verbally for you know that is where he is headed. In fact he has already arrived.

Drinking alcoholic beverages, listening to music, smoking, card playing, lipstick, makeup, hairpins, movies—all become "sins," not because the Bible has commandments against them but that they lead to sensuous living and thinking. It is interesting to note that many of the movies condemned as evil a decade ago are seen on television by the person in the dimension of the Adapted Child with little or no feeling of sin. They say that a Christian is supposed to deny pleasures in this life and to discipline the body so that brownie stamps can be earned as proof given to the self and the world that a Christian example is being set, and that one has the certainty that he is deserving of heaven.

Fundamentalism is Parent oriented. It appeals to the Adapted Child who by doing the "right" things and refraining from the "wrong" things, carefully collects brownie stamps and pastes them in the book. Fundamentalism gives the Adapted Child the authority and certainty he craves. When the book is redeemed at death, the greatest of all prizes is awarded, which is "heaven." There is much pleasure found in saving brownie stamps. The one disadvantage is that although this approach helps persons live moral and productive lives, *it is just not Christian.* Jesus neither preached nor lived a Fundamentalist life. In fact, his most outspoken critics of the first century were the religious legalists (Old Testament Fundamentalists), because Jesus' approach to life was not legalistic. He exclaimed that he did not live to do away with the law but to fulfill the law. He did not teach lawlessness; his motivation was love which causes a person to take a course of action, not because he is ordered to do it, but because he wants to do it.

The mission of Jesus was not to establish an ethical system nor to formulate a legalistic approach to heaven. His mission was to describe the kingdom of God, to proclaim that the kingdom was accessible, and that the way it was received was through the Natural Child. This is the good news, the gospel. He provided the way to the kingdom. He opened the doors of the kingdom, he leads us into the kingdom. Through his life, his death, his resurrection and his teaching he has shared the blessings of the kingdom. But this gift cannot be earned either by rational effort or self-denial. It can only be accepted by the Natural Child under the direction and supervision of the Adult.

The fundamental or conservative approach does get persons involved in programs of Bible study, worship, and devotion. Adherents are faithful in worship, study, stewardship, and discipleship. Its main appeal is to give to the Adapted Child certainty and authority, and also to give him something that he can do. But as he tries "to beat hell," he must make greater and more frequent sacrifices to prove his devotion and earn his stamps. In the process his Adapted Child has little time to relax, enjoy the scenery, and be content with life. There is little room for spontaneity, creativity, and wonder, for everything has been reduced to obedience, and obedience stifles the Natural Child. Heaven is something to be earned in the distant, misty future, but it is worth waiting for when one knows that he deserves it. The Adapted Child is found in the Roman Catholic, Eastern Orthodox, Jewish traditions, as well as many Protestant groups. No one has a corner on legalism and orthodoxy.

Another approach to the Christian faith is motivated by the Adult or reason. Here logic and humanism are companions. The will of God can be rationally determined. It is not to be found in outdated legalism or ancient creeds. Man is free to write his own credo. The liberal is concerned about pain, prejudice, poverty, and peace. Concern begins with study and ends with action. The New Testament is seen as one sourcebook for concern. Jesus is copied as the great reformer, the master social-actionist. Other authorities are also used to motivate the cleaning up of slums, combating injustice, and building the kingdom of God. Martin Luther King, Mahatma Gandhi, Martin Luther, and Albert Schweitzer are all patron saints. Form, ritual, worship, and study must give allegiance to the freedom and dignity of all men. Social action and logic are the "god-words." Marches, demonstrations, letters, politics, rallies—all bring results. God's kingdom will be built by men, almost whether God is willing or not. Here again, much good comes through this approach. Hospitals are built, slums are cleared, political shenanigans are exposed, prejudices are brought to light, drug abuse programs are formulated. The outcast, the unloved, the unclean, the untouchables are all redeemed through concern. The person, not the sin, is emphasized. Crusade and reformation are the watchwords. Adherents to this viewpoint are busy and involved.

But something is lacking. There is little Christian joy, for the Natural Child is ignored in the process. The Adult is in control and the computer is running. There is only one limitation: A computer has no feelings and whoever said the kingdom of God was going to come by computer action?

Those who go to church in the dimension of the Adult expect to find an atmosphere that is challenging to the mind but with little or no emotion being expected or shown. The logical and the scientific are stressed. Creeds are suspect, as it is believed that each person must hammer and chisel out his own statement of belief, which is based upon hard data. Expressions like "descended into hell" and "ascended into heaven" of the Apostles' Creed are without help or meaning. The truth that makes men free may be found in places outside the Old and New Testaments. God is still speaking with men. It is not uncommon for nonbiblical materials (poetry or prose) to be read aloud during the worship service. Jesus the man is stressed. The mystical, pietistic, and the magical are soft-pedaled, sometimes even rejected.

Persons who attend worship in the dimension of the Adult stress "loving and serving God with the mind." The hymns, the prayers, the sermon all talk about building the kingdom of God. The discussion group is the secret weapon of the kingdom. Committee action safeguards the democratic process and assures individuals of their rights and rewards.

People are uptight today, even people in the Christian church. Much effort is being expended, great are the budgets and many are the programs. But there is little Christian joy because the Natural Child has been ignored. There is great activity; some are fighting "sin," others "injustice." But the real Christian happiness is lacking, because the real liberation of the Natural Child has not been accomplished. The message of Jesus is to Liberate the Natural Child.

The first group is the literalist. The second group is the rationalist. A third group claims Jesus as their leader. The third classification emphasizes the Natural Child but ignores the Parent and the Adult. Emphasis is upon feeling and experience, the watchwords of existentialism. Little value is seen in either tradition or legalism. Rationality is unnecessary. What is important are results—the feelings, experiences, and "insights" a person has. This group states that little can be gained through study or following forms, ceremonies, or traditions. In fact, everything but feeling must be suspect and rejected. A careful selection of gospel and epistle teachings must be made to glean out all that supports an individual's feeling and rightness. The establishment is under careful analysis and criticism, whether the "establishment" is to be found in the church, government, or civic organization.

Anyone over thirty years of age is automatically rejected. Emphasis is upon youth, independence, feelings, relationships, and loyalties. Drugs which turn on the Natural Child may become a part of the ritual and doctrine. Conventional rules, ritual, dogma, creed, tradition, established ethics are all rejected. The emphasis is upon now, one's feelings, one's ability to experience meaningful relationships. In one respect it may be a reaction against formalism, but it is also a desire to fulfill a real and pressing need to express and find one's self. Adherents to this approach to living demand to be heard.

Since feeling is the "god-word," at the expense of orthodoxy (Parent) and reason (Adult), some uninhibited extremes have resulted.

The Natural Child calls the shots without the benefit of either the Parent or Adult discipline. The resulting synthesis has been hero worship of some pretty eccentric personages, emotionalism, questionable doctrine, weird rituals, an ethical system based upon expediency and selfishness, ignorance of basic facts of the life of Jesus, a deliberate selection of certain biblical happenings to the exclusion of those that are contrary to their position, a rejection of generally accepted authorities and scholars, and emphasis upon "speaking in tongues" and the leadership of the Holy Spirit.

The Natural Child is liberated but is unsupervised and undisciplined. The end result of this freewheeling system will be chaos and disaster. Hopefully the Adult may demand to be heard, and will get about the business of data processing and supervision. If this can happen then a stability and permanence may be given to this group.

The desirable and appropriate dimension for going to church is the same one for family and community living: the Adult in control, which silences the Parent when it is stifling, then deliberately liberates the Natural Child who is then able to respond to the love of God and the love of man. The Natural Child, though, needs always to be under constant supervision by the Adult. This dimension permits the worshiper to worship God in "spirit" (Natural Child) and in "truth" (Adult).

This writer is desirous not of starting a new denomination, but of isolating the shortcomings and sicknesses of present-day Christianity by using the technique of Transactional Analysis to recapture the message and spirit of the church in the first century, as well as the personality and spirit of the founder, Jesus Christ. These insights can be applied by any Christian in any church or denomination, in any century. It can also be the motivation for a new approach to the ecumenical movement. Put the Adult in control. Turn off the Parent when the inputs are a hindrance (which also silences the Adapted Child) and then, under Adult supervision, liberate the Natural Child—the only dimension that can experience the joy Jesus Christ came to share abundantly.

The worship service is approached by the Adult who has much recorded data verifying that church attendance and study can give a stability and meaning to life that is rarely found elsewhere. The Adult in control goes to church, moreover, out of desire and need, not *just* for new data about God and doing God's will but to share the worship experience with other "brothers and sisters" in the family of God. The Adult has learned that the Christian faith is not just a "cooked up" scheme to bleed money out of the pockets of victims, nor is it a place frequented only by weaklings, misfits, malcontents, cowards, and namby-pamby "Milquetoasts."

With the Adult in control a person searches from place to place until he finds a church that he can enter without feeling hypocritical. It may be that he will have to continue this search for some period of time. Few churches today are oriented to have the Adult in control, which can then liberate the Natural Child to worship, to expect miracles of faith to happen, to know the wonderful presence of the Holy Spirit, to give expression of the Natural Child in order to respond to the love of God in song, fellowship, sacrament, scripture, prayer, sermon, the peace and to join with others, not only in worship, but in community and worldwide witnessing of the faith. The worship service is not something he periodically observes, but an experience he shares with God and man. The church helps him put together the jigsaw puzzle of life, giving him insights and inspiration.

The Christian life is not a sponge that soaks up the love of God for one's own enjoyment and security; it is a "regrouping" experience to find new dimensions of reality and service. The symbol is not the rocking chair but a piece of electrical conduit, connected to the power of God at one end and the needs of the world at the other. Anything that interrupts or short-circuits the flow of energy must be logically removed and repairs made.

When the Natural Child is liberated in this environment and supervised by the Adult, then the expectancy and wonder of the Natural Child can be liberated. The Natural Child expects God to give him a revelation. The "OK CHILD" is open to the Holy Spirit. He is filled with wonder, enthusiasm, generosity, expectancy, love, spontaneity, and faith. When he prays, it is the prayer of the "OK CHILD." When he receives the sacraments, it is the "OK CHILD" who projects meaning and feeling into the symbols. When he sings, when he gives his offering, when he enjoys fellowship with others, when he gives the peace, when he shares the love of God, when he listens to the sermon, it is as the "OK CHILD" being supervised by the Adult. When the call to discipleship comes, he, like the disciples of the first century, responds in the dimension of the Natural Child.

Miracles of faith are anticipated and recognized. There are "signs" and "wonders" to be experienced and shared. The power, love, and grace of God did not become depleted because of abuse or misuse in the first century. This is one fact of life that needs no conservation program.

The more it is desired and used, the more there will be available and the quality will even be increased. The more it is hoarded or selfishly administered the less and less it becomes, finally fading completely away. The Natural Child expects the sick to be healed, the sorrowful to be comforted, the lost to be found, the unloved to be loved. The church is the focal point of God's revelation to man. It is in the dimension of the "OK CHILD" that the person receives the love and grace of God. It is the heavenly sunlight of God's beautiful concern for humans magnified and focused upon lives responsive to the light. The "OK CHILD" is not compelled to measure and explain the religious experience scientifically. Its value is in the experience itself. Like the love between husband and wife it is enjoyed, not analyzed. To attempt rationally to explain love or prove its existence is of little consequence, either to the one who has known love before or to the one who refuses to love. The love of God for man and the love of man for God is reality and truth. To have any meaning, though, it has to be experienced.

Just as there were hang-ups in the New Testament church, so there are imperfections in the modern church. When the church becomes Authority (Parent), Library (Adult), or Source of brownie stamps (Adapted Child), some distortions come about. When the Natural Child lacks supervision by the Adult, the church becomes chaotic and noisy. The church today can get hung up on orthodoxy and authority, more concerned about mechanics than the end product. The church may also take the tangent of the "NOT OK CHILD" trying to collect sufficient brownie stamps to prove dedication and obedience. The church may be a forum where many facts are considered and decisions reached. But, unless it is the "OK CHILD" who approaches his Father and other members of the family, under the supervision of the Adult, great projects may be completed but there is little joy in the process. Joy is the "nitty-gritty" of the Christian faith and can only be experienced by the Natural Child.

In church groups where the intimacy of relationships is experienced under the direction of the Adult dimension, some beautiful and meaningful experiences have resulted. Cell groups, encounter groups, study groups, fellowship groups—all have resulted in the deepening of understanding regarding the Christian faith but have often been the fertile soil where the meaning of the New Testament church is recaptured and relived. Not only does the head (Adult) dimension profit from such discipline but the heart (Natural Child) is liberated and encouraged to enjoy life. Lives are changed, relationships become more fulfilling, life becomes beautiful when people can approach each other in the dimension of the "OK CHILD" under Adult supervision. The church is a natural place for these encounters, for this whole approach to life was originated by Jesus of Nazareth, for persons living in the first and every century.

9

The Dimension That Takes
the Clergy to Church

An effective way to determine which dimension is in control in a
situation is to look for emotion. If emotion is being shown then it is
apparent that the person is either coming through in the dimension of
the Child or the Parent. The Adult comes through as a data processor,
interested only in facts. A computer does not get emotional. The
nonverbals, as well as the verbals, are important factors to be observed.
The choice of words, the tone of voice, gestures, facial expression are all
important details to be noticed.

The approach to liturgics and preaching by the clergy is notewor-
thy. Whether a clergyman feels "OK" or "NOT OK" and what he
thinks about God and people will be reflected in his life-style and
ministry.

This information is helpful to ascertain the dimension that clergy
take to church. The clergy have often been labeled as "God's angry
men," who are usually uptight about some condition or weakness. Many
find it easy to speak "for" God, pronouncing his judgment, standards,
will. Others are content to talk about God sticking to "factual" data.

Isaiah, the prophet, counseled, "Come now, let us reason together
(Isa. 1:18)." This is the dimension of the Adult who is anxious to deal
with the facts. Some clergy enter a worship service in this dimension.
Reason and logic are primary virtues. People who are like-minded find
this approach to life meaningful and helpful. This stems from an "I'M

OK—YOU'RE OK" life-style which keeps an optimistic outlook on the world and relationships. This does not mean that evil is ignored or soft-pedaled. But the clergy are not hung up on sin and the personification of evil lurking in the shadows ready to consume persons in an unguarded moment. They recognize the goodness as well as the badness in people. They remain generally optimistic about man's ability to progress, build, solve problems, and bring about a better world. They cite many illustrations of men who have had "visions" of a new world of relationships, and these have become realities. What is needed, these clergymen feel, is education, democratic action, honest evaluation of life, individual worth and potential, the spark of godliness that is within every person. The church is the assembly place for concerned people. The worship service is the rallying point for community action. The scripture lessons, hymns, prayers, sermons all carry the theme of analysis and action. The time is now. Heaven is not some far off distant place but a reality here and now wherever people live together as brothers. Hell is present in this life and is an audiovisual reminder of man's inhumanity and greed. If people cannot live in the here and now it is doubtful whether they will desire each other's company in the hereafter.

A liberal education of the clergy is stressed, including graduate courses in literature, composition, languages, sociology, psychology, philosophy, political science, history, and economics. Concentration on religion and biblical courses takes place in seminary where courses are offered on a graduate level. A clergyman trained in this Adult dimension will probably enter the church on Sunday morning in the Adult dimension. The designation "preacher" only describes one part of his approach in worship. He could equally be called "liturgist" or "pray-er" for he understands that no one part of worship is to be emphasized over another part. The sermon is not necessarily the most important part of worship, although he carefully prepares before entering the pulpit. But he also carefully prepares the liturgy and prayers. The order of service is well organized before he ever enters the church to conduct it. The hymns, scripture selections, sermon material—all are selected with a definite theme in mind. To the clergy in the Adult dimension the purpose of a worship service is not to "save souls" but to educate and to provide an environment for fellowship and praise. The clergyman is not motivated by a legalistic "thou shalt" approach, but out of the commandment to love God with the total personality. Worship begins on Sunday but lasts throughout the week in the way a person lives his life. Living is worship.

The foregoing is the clergyman going to church in the dimension of the Adult. Another dimension that a clergyman can be in when he enters the house of God is the Adapted Child, also called the "NOT OK" Child. He, like the laymen in this dimension, is a brownie stamp saver. He goes to church for the same reason as his layman counterpart. (This is discussed in the previous chapter "Which Dimension Takes You to Church?") He feels unworthy, but he hopes that he can become worthy and he drives himself feverishly to accumulate a large number of brownie stamps to prove his devotion and loyalty. In fact, this is his reason for going into the ministry. Look at his sacrifice; look what he gave up; look how humble he is; look how deserving he is. He never hesitates to tell people about his accomplishments and sacrifices. He is proud of it. Like one clergyman told the author, "I'm proud of my humility." Humility is a Christian virtue, but a *display* of humility is disgusting, repulsive and unchristian. Persons in the dimension of the Adapted Child crave orthodoxy and authority. They need to have vivid standards and rules so they can have the certainty they need to evaluate their progress. They stick to the "fundamentals"; they obey the "rules"; they deny the body; they discipline the senses; they test the spirit; they guard the orthodoxy. They play the Game "Mine's Better Than Yours," although underneath there is a secret fear that they may not be "good enough" or that they may not have quite enough brownie stamps to get the coveted prize.

Clergy in the dimension of the Adapted Child offer a number of worship services, stressing the need for midweek services as well as worship on Sunday morning and evening. There is also a great need to have periodic concentrated series of evangelistic services where visiting authority figures can give the motivation for continued brownie stamp collecting as well as whet the appetites for greater and better prizes offered at the redemption center.

Worship services conducted by clergymen in the "NOT OK" Child dimension take on a bizarre atmosphere. Such a clergyman sees himself as a man of unclean lips and heart dwelling in the midst of people who are similarly constructed. Sin, evil, corruption, greed, sensuousness, temptation, weakness, imperfection are the facts of this life. To make matters worse they are personified in a tempter who is always lurking in the shadows ready to attack a person in an unguarded moment. To prevent compromise such a person must not only arm himself with brownie stamps to combat the opposition but also have an authority figure lead him in the battle and give him motivation to remain faithful until the end. The sermon, prayers, hymns, scripture lesson—all are designed to aid in this struggle. The worship service is an assembly of "NOT OK" persons who have a great motivation to become "OK." The sermon is the most important part of worship as it counsels both the "NOT OK" laymen and the "NOT OK" preacher to be diligent in stamp collecting; how and where to shop for brownie stamps; what is offered at the redemption center; and the necessity for faithfulness to God as well as alertness to the devil's power. These "NOT OK" clergymen are often called "preachers" and they accept this title as descriptive of their calling. Their preaching is rooted in authority (the fundamentals). Since their inner struggle is with "NOT OK-ness" they continually preach about the struggles within, sin, sensuousness, and lust. Their training is based upon authority. Their goals are assured by authority.

Clergymen who enter the church in the dimension of the Adapted or "NOT OK" Child are to be found many places. Their motivation transcends denominations. The means to the end may vary but the end is the same: to earn salvation by selfless, fervent dedication. As one examines various denominations one sees varying colors of brownie stamps offered by different groups; but they are all obtained through orthodoxy and authority by those in the "NOT OK" Child dimension.

A third dimension for the clergy entering the church for worship is that of the Parent, the lawgiver, the rulegiver, the authority figures, the judge, the spokesman, the prophet. The motivation in comparison to the Adapted Child who is "NOT OK" is that the clergyman in the Parent dimension feels "OK." His life-style is "I'M OK—YOU'RE NOT OK" but you can become "OK" if you . . . The Christian faith comes by prescription from one who is "smarter" than the people. This clergyman has certainty, truth, and direction. There is a trinity of sin, satan, and salvation. He dispenses the word with authority and urgency. The prophet's training and calling give him the credentials to diagnose the symptoms of the people and direct the "medication." "Take this," "do this," "believe this," "forsake this," "avoid this." When he stands in the pulpit or counsels in his office he comes through as "I'M OK—YOU'RE NOT OK—but you can be OK if you . . . believe what I tell you, do what I say, jump when I say jump, fear what I tell you, avoid what I direct; and in the process you will get brownie stamps to show your progress." He has advice for every situation, answers for every question, certainty for every anxiety.

The Parent-oriented clergyman needs to minister to "NOT OK" people, and "NOT OK" people need to have the authority of a Parent clergyman. They need each other. They augment each other and give meaning to each other's lives. The clergyman is a strange hybrid of the judge and the cheerleader. He is not the shepherd who leads the sheep but the shepherd who drives the sheep. He does not share the vicissitudes of the flock for he has risen above the struggle. He has overcome. The people struggle in the valley, but he is upon the mountain, broadcasting advice, instruction, and encouragement. He has special knowledge and resources. He is set apart from the people. He encourages sacrifice, discipline, and restraint but he seems to not be bound by these forces.

Perhaps this pastor began his religious quest from the Adapted Child position, but his brownie stamp book is large and completely full of stamps. Though he has little motivation to save more stamps he admonishes the "NOT OK" people to continue to do so. The worship service is the place where brownie stamp collecting is emphasized, where the appetite is whetted for the prizes offered at the redemption center. The whole tone of the service is to diagnose the sickness of men and give prescriptions for healing. Not only are there vivid descriptions of the valuable prizes offered by the redemption center, but also what will happen to those persons who reject brownie stamp collecting. The penalty for the rejection of the Parent-Adapted Child approach is to "go to hell," and suffer for eternity all the pains and tortures of disobedience. The temperature of the place and the type of treatment in hell cause many an Adapted Child to jump through the hoops of orthodoxy in hopes of getting an angry and demanding Parent off his back. It is suggested that one reason why some persons submit to "conversion" is to please not only the Parent within but also the Parent in the pulpit. The "NOT OK" Child can hope for a little peace only by obeying the demands of the Parent. But, like one who tries to find a little pleasure by giving in to a little temptation, the "NOT OK" Child begins a frustrating life of trying to save enough brownie stamps to earn "OK-ness"; the more brownie stamps he saves the more he sees he needs to save.

If Transactional Analysis is a dependable tool for evaluating relationships and motivations, then it should be a helpful aid in determining the most appropriate dimension for a clergyman to be in when he enters the church and performs his ministry. Having the Adult in control to assemble and evaluate data in order to control the Parent and also to liberate the Natural Child—this is the most effective as well as the most fulfilling dimension for the clergyman. To be able to understand the truth about God and man and then share the truth with others in a simple and meaningful way is a beautiful calling. This was the motivation and calling of Jesus, and should be the motivation and calling of those who minister in his name. It is important that a clergyman know what life on the mountain is all about (orthodoxy and legalism), but unless he lives and walks with the people he serves, unless he can laugh and cry with them, meet with them, relate with them, share their hopes and fears, their struggles and their aspirations, their pain and their uncertainties, he will have a lonely life and will ill equip the people to face life and living. The most helpful and fruitful life-style of the clergyman is the "I'M OK—YOU'RE OK" position. From this perspective he and his congregation can face reality with optimism and victory. It is easy for the congregation to discover the life-style and approach of their minister.

Worship should be not a painful but a mentally challenging and emotionally fulfilling experience. People, including clergymen, need to find fulfillment in worship that inspires rather than strangulates, that leads rather than drives, that encourages rather than orders, that attracts "OK" people for both the pulpit and the pew. These were the goals of Jesus and they should be the motivation for his ministers.

The last decade has seen a number of the clergy become discouraged, disillusioned, and depressed about performing their ministry. Often the blame has been placed upon the congregation who are "unresponsive or unappreciative or unchristian." It is suggested that most of the problem was due to the approach of the clergyman: what he thought of himself, and why he felt he should perform a ministry in the first place. What dimension was he in when he decided to be a minister? Why did he want to go into the ministry? Which of the four possible life-styles did he possess? ("I'M OK—YOU'RE OK," "I'M OK—YOU'RE NOT OK," "I'M NOT OK—YOU'RE OK," "I'M NOT OK—YOU'RE NOT OK.") The only healthy approach to the ministry is that life-style personified by Jesus: "I'M OK—YOU'RE OK." If it were important for Jesus to feel "OK" and to live among "OK" people, can his representative in this century do less? To be able to feel "OK" does not come about just by getting an education or doing field work.

"OK-ness" is a response to the love of God in the dimension of the Natural Child. It cannot be faked or counterfeited. Like love in any relationship, love in ministry has to be experienced to be understood. It is suggested that many persons ordained in the church have tried to share something with others that they did not possess themselves. There is a great difference between talking about love and experiencing love. All the right "God-words" can be carefully selected and used but unless the speaker has experienced love, the words are like "a noisy gong or a clanging cymbal (1 Cor. 13:1)." Unless the minister has a liberated Natural Child that has experienced the grace and love of God, his words and his ministry will be hollow, ineffective, and unfulfilling. Worship services conducted by either the Parent or the Adapted Child may do a little good; some persons seem to be programed to respond to life and worship from the "NOT OK" position. Worship services led by the Adult—where only logic, facts and the gift of reason are expounded— may be challenging to some who approach life through the Adult. But, unless the qualities of the Natural or "OK Child" are personified by both the liturgist and the laymen, the love and grace of God will never become a reality.

Love is the basic ingredient of God and man. There is no substitute for it on either the divine or the human level. It must be a responsible love, that is, it must be undergirded and supervised by the Adult. This was the usual dimension of Jesus. This should be the usual dimension of his representative who ministers in the pulpit and at the altar. The sign and seal of this dimension of life is joy—the quality of living Jesus talked about, personified, and gave his life to make a reality for men. It can come only to those persons who personify an "I'M OK—YOU'RE OK" life-style, which is the appropriate motivation for the Christian, whether he is in the pulpit or pew. This motivation cannot be turned on and off at will. It is not a dimension that is activated for an hour on Sunday morning. It needs to be the total approach of a person.

There is no such thing as a "part-time" Christian. Some speak of going into "full-time Christian service," which means becoming some sort of a professional in the ministry of the church. But whether a person is ordained or not, the Christian faith needs to captivate the whole person in all three dimensions and in all relationships of life. It is a phony who talks about love in the church and then turns into a monster and ogre in the home; it is a hypocrite who speaks of faith in the church and then anxiously worries about the security of food, drink, and lodging; it is an "actor" who speaks about his conversion in the church and then whines, complains, and loses his temper in the home. Unless the person can live the Christian life in his daily relationships, then his religion is a lie, a sham, and a veneer. Many women who are married to clergyman must walk a tightrope between what the mate preaches in the church and what he practices in the home. If there is such a thing as a "congressional medal" to be given in heaven, those first in line will be wives married to those clergymen who don't practice what they preach. For a clergyman who cannot maintain an "I'M OK—YOU'RE OK" life-style in the parsonage with his wife and family is a fake, a fraud, and a cheat.

The most significant and the most fulfilling ministry in the church for both the clergyman and the people he serves is from the "I'M OK—YOU'RE OK" position, where the Adult has evaluated the Parental inputs and silenced the Parent where it was inappropriate; and where the Natural Child is liberated yet supervised. The qualities of the Natural Child are as important for the minister to take to church as for the laymen. These are: openness, enthusiasm, expectancy, wonder, responsiveness, lack of prejudice, creativity, spontaneousness, self-abandonment, imagination, receptivity, faith, love, and hope. The approach to worship should be through the "OK" emotions with the mind supervising the experience and keeping it appropriate. The Christian faith is a "heart" not a "head" religion, although the "head" is the supervisor. Leaders of worship need to be able to be responsive to the love of God and love of fellowman in the dimension of the "OK" Child of God who goes to church not out of fear or obligation or habit, but out of love. The throne of grace is approached not with brownie stamps but with "OK-ness" and acceptance. The "OK Child" naturally turns to his "OK Heavenly Father" because of the love and trust relationship. This is a responsible (Adult supervised) love, divine and the human. Without supervision the Natural Child could bring about confusion and chaos. Worship could become noisy, flamboyant, lascivious, and chaotic. All kinds of strange and contradictory practices could creep into the church under the uninhibited sensuousness of the Natural Child if there is no supervision by the Adult.

Worship of God can be experienced in any of the three dimensions of personality. But the one that is most responsive to the love of God is the Natural Child who is undergirded and under surveillance by the Adult. If the clergy can accomplish this miracle of faith they will be in a wonderful position for God to speak to them and through them and thus encourage the laymen not only to come to church in the same dimension but also to have the potential for Christian devotion and discipleship.

10

Modern Attempts
to Liberate the Child

Each generation has felt the need to liberate the child. The present generation is no exception. "Parent-orientation" or "Adult-orientation" may produce societies that are productive and monumental but unless the Natural Child can play and find enjoyment, life lacks meaning and fulfillment.

Modern people are living in an age which not only dreams of visiting outer space but also makes this a reality. We build machinery which sends men to the moon and brings them back with samples to analyze and evaluate. We harness the atom and unlock its secrets of power and potential. We convert the vast resources of this earth into energy and design equipment that in a limited way controls the environment, making it desirable and comfortable. We analyze the soil and bring out its greatest potential.

Yet our needs and desires always seem to be ahead of our ability to produce and distribute. In some areas we have inventions that make living easier, yet a substance as normally common as fresh water is not available in sufficient quantities because of pollution and greed. Our automatic washers of dishes and clothes sometimes stand idle for lack of this basic ingredient. The air round us which has been long taken for granted by mankind now becomes of great concern when cities pollute the atmosphere and end up with smog and foul air. Humans must constantly push forward to new and better ways of coping with the natural resources of the earth. Man must be in control or else this world will cease to be a habitable place. Where will we go if we cannot live here?

The Adult (Reason) must stay in control. It must plan and produce. The Parent must establish and enforce laws which assure the distribution of the basics of life including equality, justice, and freedom for all men. It can no longer be taken for granted that persons in succeeding generations will automatically have enough to sustain life. There must be planning, there must be concern, there must be enforcement. The Adult must be in control to plan and use the natural resources of the world.

The environment must be found to be friendly as well as productive. This friendly feeling is experienced through the Natural Child and must be present or all other resources and developments are of little account. Various ways of producing friendliness and fulfillment will be discussed in this chapter. A man will strive to be happy even if he has to counterfeit happiness; the ways the modern man attempts to liberate the Child artificially will be discussed in this chapter.

CHEMICAL CULTURE

The late 1900's is a chemical culture. There is a pill or drug for everything. If you want to be "up" or "down," awake or asleep, high or low, expand the mind or become more sociable, relax, find enjoyment or peace or tranquility or escape or release, the place to find it, many people say, is in some sort of a drug as panacea. This motivation transcends age, ethnic or social bounds. The person drinking twelve cups of coffee a day and the glue-sniffer have the use of drugs in common. The one who blows grass and the two-martinis-before-dinner drinker are similarly motivated. Those who get hooked on sleeping pills, diet pills, and stimulants are to be found in all age groups.

The wino, the social drinker, the beer guzzler, the drunk, the potential alcoholic all have a common denominator; they all seek the drugging effect of alcohol. They drink alcohol, not generally because of the taste, but because of the effect it brings. They return to the bottle to recapture a feeling or experience.

Those who use pot, pills, or other chemicals to bring about a change in body chemistry and hence some sort of feeling all are using artificial means to liberate the Child. The Natural Child wants to and needs to be liberated. The Parent and the Adapted Child are so powerful that in order for the persons to have any sensual pleasure, the Parent and Adapted Child have to be anesthetized or put to sleep so the Natural Child can find some momentary peace. While the drug is in effect there is some pleasure. But the liberation of the Child through drug abuse is only a temporary oasis. In addition a person can become physically and/or psychologically addicted to the drug. Then the person is apt to forget the real reason for the return to the drug, and its use is only filling a need rather than a fulfillment.

The person who uses tobacco begins for a variety of reasons: the thing to do, relieve monotony, find pleasure, a kick, like the taste, etc., but many smokers continue to smoke, not for pleasure but for habit and addiction. To watch a person addicted to cigarettes pour out one, light it up and inhale several deep draughts is to see someone who appears to find great pleasure and satisfaction. Yet a person may repeat the ritual with little awareness of what is happening. It may become sheer habit and ritual. It is interesting to watch a smoker fondle his "connection" while he uses it but when he is finished he extinguishes it with real vengeance or flips it as far as he can as though he is really angry at the weed as well as the habit. Yet he returns to the drug in a few minutes to repeat the ritual.

The younger generation is often advertised as the "unhooked generation." This is not true. It is a hooked generation, perhaps more than the seniors or at least as much as the seniors. But it *is* a hooked generation. It is a drug-dependent generation, with an assortment of drugs far wider than the parents and grandparents ever had available. There is a difference. The younger generation has fewer hang-ups from drug abuse and more openness than any other generation as they were born into a drug culture. They accept it. They have a broad knowledge of what is available legally, what the effects of different drugs are, what the penalties for possession and use of illegal drugs are, and how and where to secure the drugs if they are desired. Suppliers are handy as well as the funds to purchase them. Many homes have an open bar where alcoholic drinks are available to unsupervised young people. The choice to turn on or not to turn on with drugs is one that young people face many times during the day. Their peers do, and their seniors do, so why shouldn't they? And many of them do. Young people see no difference between socially smoking marijuana and socially having mixed drinks.

It is interesting that many drug abuse programs formulated by older persons (who live in their own chemical culture) tend to use two approaches with little success: (1) The drug information program with the identification and description of effects of various drugs and (2) the "scare" technique seem nearly worthless to motivate a young person to refrain from using drugs. Young people can identify and are aware of the effects of various drugs. Frequently they know far more about drug abuse than their seniors. The scare approach which was used with questionable results with the troops during World War II on the subject of VD has little noticeable effect on young persons today, any more than showing a drunken bum asleep in a doorway to a two-martinis-before-dinner drinker, in an attempt to make him pledge a life of abstinence.

People seem to use drugs to turn off the Parent and give the Adult a rest, so that the Natural Child can play. One who comes under the control of the drug shows obvious "signs" of the Child. Sometimes the hurtful, spiteful, hateful, selfish, "NOT OK" Adapted Child is released when one is under the influence of drugs, making the person some kind of a monster. In this condition he is unable to function as a mature, considerate, and meaningful person, nor is he any fun to be around. In fact the person seems not to be having fun, and certainly the persons who must relate with him are handicapped in their enjoyment of life by his antics.

It is the opinion of the writer that persons use drugs to try to turn on the Natural Child and to find some momentary enjoyment and happiness. It is an artificially induced euphoria brought about through chemicals. To generalize about the effects of drugs is hazardous, as there is such a range and variation in the drug spectrum. There is a difference between the "lift" that comes from smoking cigarettes and taking a trip on LSD; a difference comparing the cup of coffee with an injection of heroin, the cold bottle of 3.2 beer with the quart consumption of 90-proof vodka, the glass of wine at dinner time with some of the hair of the dog that bit you the night before. Yet, all are used to "encourage" the Natural Child to come out of hiding and find some enjoyment in life.

There is a staggering amount of drugs consumed today. Billions of dollars are spent annually on various medications. Many of these drugs have been placed on the market to relieve pain and help people cope with life. When they are used to restore health, bring out the best in the person, make him a better father, husband, neighbor, provider, and member of the human race, then the use of drugs may be justified. But when they bring unhappiness, death, injury, lawlessness, tragedy, disease, destruction, pain, waste, and slow or rapid suicide, their use needs to be questioned and stopped.

In terms of Transactional Analysis there is a need for the Adult to ascertain the facts, to seek out all the information that can be learned about drugs, their use and abuse. The Adult must also examine the material collected by the Parent and modify false information. There is no value in ignorance of drug abuse or any other subject. The need for the drug must be analyzed and a rational application made. The Adult must see the pressing need for the Natural Child to be liberated perhaps in other more fruitful and less damaging ways. The Adult can remove the need for the person to get bombed or stoned on drugs by substituting more reasonable ways for the Natural Child to be expressed and exercised. Would it not be a great achievement to be able to liberate the Natural Child through more fulfilling and less damaging ways?

Eric Berne, in his book *Games People Play*, sees alcohol abuse as a "Game." * This Game is not played for fun but for a payoff which is the "hangover." There are others who may play the Game with the victim: the "Persecutor," the "Rescuer," the "Patsy or Dummy," and the "Connection." The person who plays this Game or other Games related to alcohol ("Martini" and "Morning After") is looking for "strokes." He desperately needs to be noticed, to be accepted as a person, even to be castigated and put down, if this is the only way he can obtain his recognition.

Claude Steiner sees the alcoholic as being locked in with a self-destructive life script which he wrote early in his life.† This script or life plan was written by the Adult of the young person, often before all the facts were determined. Incorporated in the script are not only inputs from authority figures in the home and church but also early experiences in satisfying his needs and expectation. A "NOT OK" feeling in the Adapted Child formulates guideposts for later living. Therapy involves examination of the script with a conscious effort in the Adult dimension to turn it off when it is harmful and to substitute a more satisfying and fulfilling plan of life.

Alcohol, then, is used by persons to silence the Parent by anesthetizing its strangulating control upon the Adapted Child in order for the Adapted Child to have some momentary peace. Alcohol may also be used to create situations where attention is focused upon the person

---

* Eric Berne, *Games People Play* (New York: Grove Press, 1964), p. 73.
† Claude Steiner, *Games Alcoholics Play* (New York: Grove Press, 1971), p. 32.

even if the strokes so obtained are critical and damaging. In either case it can be a technique to release the person from the struggle within between the Parent and the "NOT OK" Child. It is an attempt to "free the Child" so that some peace, pleasure, or release from conflict can come within.

To get a "glow" on is an attempt to get the Parent off one's back and to somehow feel "OK." Sometimes, though, when the Parent and the Adult are both trussed and silenced, the "NOT OK" Child comes out without any supervision or control. This person, regardless of age, not only becomes an obnoxious, ugly, spoiled brat but is quite incapable of dealing with right and wrong, good and bad, reasonable and unreasonable. Once Pandora's box is opened by the drug the brat comes out to wreak havoc on his life and the lives of other persons.

It is true that some persons are able to release the "OK" Child when they drink alcohol. These seem to be able to relax, enjoy life, laugh, have fun, be sociable, do funny dances, say humorous things, sing, tell stories, clown around, become loving, release inhibitions, remove walls and barriers. For a few minutes or hours the world looks better, life is beautiful, living is fun. But several drawbacks are always present. Persons in this condition may be incapable of assuming the role of father, mother, husband, or wife; they have a distorted conception of their well-being, control, and abilities; they may be unable to make a logical decision based on facts, drive an automobile or motorcycle safely, avoid a dangerous life and death situation. When the Adult loses control these people are about as effective as six-year-old children. This is often the basis for accidents on the freeway, breakdown in marriage or family relationships, absurd positions taken on issues, and foolish decisions on important subjects. Character assassination may take place; people can still be hurt in personality or limb, insulted, abused, ignored, or forgotten by the drunken person. Only the selfish needs and desires of the individual are turned on, often at the expense of others, particularly those in the family relationship. Alcohol continues to be a crutch, often causing permanent and serious injury to many more than the victim.

Drug abuse in the realm of illegal or unnecessary pills, powders, and syringes continues to cripple and incapacitate millions in this century. These victims are often the young and immature. Yet, the motivation is frequently the same as that which causes Mom and Dad to use socially accepted drug abuse methods. Whether a person is "stoned" on pills or "smashed" on booze the symptoms and motivations are similar.

The "Games" Dr. Berne describes are not played for fun. They are a substitute for intimate living. When people can express themselves at gut level, both speaking and hearing, this relationship can be so satisfying that there will be small need for counterfeiting "strokes." The road to intimate living is through the Adult taking control, dealing with facts, making responsible choices based on facts, turning the Parent off when its inputs are damaging, and then liberating the Natural Child under the supervision of the Adult. In an emergency situation the Adult can take immediate control and put appropriate action into effect.

SEXUAL REVOLUTION

When the present age is analyzed and evaluated by future historians it is suspected that the 1960's and 1970's will be known as the period of the great sexual revolution. The sexual makeup of persons and the resulting intimate sexual contacts have always been a basic part of life. Today sex is emphasized and exploited to such an extent that it seems to be the tail that wags the dog of life. The symbol for the present age may well be a pair of magnificently shaped feminine breasts which hold many males and not a few females spellbound with admiring appreciation. What once had great functional value to nourish humanity, giving security to both sexes, now has become the expedient for arousing and holding intense interest. It is the Natural Child that finds pleasure either in viewing or displaying the breasts or some other part of the human anatomy. That bare breasts can be openly shown on the movie screen, in books, magazines, and newspapers, and even on the television screen is illustrative of the fact that the majority of persons today evidently enjoy the view.

For many years the nude human form was considered to be vulgar and the sexual parts "dirty." Consequently in countries where Parent-Adapted Child ethics were enforced, the laws and customs dictated that the body be covered. The "costumes" worn at the beaches by "bathers" in the early 1900's were extreme efforts not only to be modest but to annihilate the difference between the sexes, producing some sort of a neuter gender. There were exceptions to this rule, though, when ladies in fashion wore low-cut dresses to display their breasts, false bottoms to accentuate their buttocks, and corsets to push their anatomy to upper or lower levels.

Today the emphasis is upon the natural look. What used to be grossly distorted is now seen as normal and beautiful. A revolution has come in the attitude toward and acceptance of sex. The motivation for the liberation of the Child in the sexual revolution comes from the dimension of the Adult rejecting the Parental guidelines. One group gives the Natural Child "laissez-faire," the other group uses the Adult to supervise the new sexual freedom.

When the Natural Child is uncontrolled some flagrant practices and positions may be released. It is the Adult that must be involved in supervising the Natural Child or there can be few responsible decisions and efforts. In sexual practices as in other areas of life there must be the undergirding of Adult responsibility, or else persons are seen as playthings to be used or rejected as one feels at the moment.

A young man or lady may have a casual and open attitude toward having sex. They may have sexual intercourse even before they know each other's names. "Sex is pleasurable; sex is fun; I'm taking the pill so there is no chance of pregnancy, so let's ball!" And so they use each other's bodies to simulate the pleasure of sex. Things seem exciting for a time but sexual promiscuity may eventually take its toll in insecurity, guilt, fear, and a general feeling of "NOT OK-ness."

The danger of a revolution is that, as the Natural Child attempts to free life from the choking grasp of the Parent, all the Parental material is discarded with no controls or standards inserted in its place. The baby is thrown out with the bath water. The rule for living becomes pleasure for the moment, in large and exciting dimensions, in many and varied ways. An illustration of this is to be found in movie theaters today. When the "bare bust barrier" on film was broken fifteen years ago the door was opened to expose more and more. It is now expected that unless a major movie has several scenes where the leading actor and actress are engaged in sexual intercourse in living color and stereophonic sound, the movie does not have a chance to make the box office. The Natural Child of the public demands more exciting and realistic scenes and practices. What do you show after the public finds commonplace and dull the endless positions of intercourse; where the camera catches every realistic movement and contact; with multiple confrontations in beds and in the fields, with an assortment of every known sexual technique with the same or opposite sex; where animals and children become involved in the confrontations; where it is clear that the actors are not acting and the actresses are not actressing, but that it's the real thing, in dynamic, pulsating, genuine lust? The voyeur has plenty of respectable places to visit—the stage, screen, and night clubs—to titillate the curiosity of his Natural Child and tickle the billfolds of the Natural

Child actors. Formerly it was believed that only a depraved person would have an appetite for such programing but the sexual revolution has made it clear that persons in many walks of life enjoy this type of show.

Whether sexual encounters take place at a more frequent rate *before* marriage, or whether there are more *extra*marital affairs today is up for discussion. There have always been these kinds of outlets and relationships by the uncontrolled and undisciplined Natural Child. It is felt by many that the encounters today are more open, more publicized, and generally more tolerated by moderns. The pill and the pad have given a freedom of sexual expression that was not generally available before. But sex without responsibility is not an invention of the sixties and seventies; it has been around as long as man and woman.

The girl in the dimension of the Natural Child who wears hot pants must be willing to assume some of the responsibility of giving "hot pants" to the Natural Child of a man who may not have Parental or Adult supervision to control his aggressiveness. The girl who wears see-through blouses without the benefit of a bra must be willing to assume at least half of the responsibility that the Natural Child of a man may become so curious that he may force her to show more. Men who wear skin-tight trousers should not be surprised when the opposite (and sometimes the same) sex shows more than a passing interest in what he is wearing and how it fits. How a person dresses, what styles and cuts are worn, appeals in the dimension of Natural Child. A person dresses as he feels, and clothing or the absence of clothing is of interest to the Natural Child.

Sex is here to stay. In many respects the Sexual Revolution has brought about some helpful, enjoyable, and healthy reforms. But in sexual relations, as in all human transactions, the Natural Child's response to sex must be monitored by the Adult.

RELIGIOUS TANGENTS

One of the modern attempts to liberate the child, expecially for young people, is to turn to religion. Religion here is not defined as the traditional and the orthodox, but the occult and the mysterious. In the search for intimacy, self-realization, and self-fulfillment, a variety of experiences are sought. As with so many methods that young people choose to liberate the Child, there are certain benefits that come in return. Turning to untraditional approaches, to mysticism, they derive the excitement of discovering new data and methods concerning the unknown; they are able to identify with their peers who share their new discoveries; and in the process they irritate and threaten the status of persons in the establishment.

The traditional approaches to religion are suspected by the revolutionists of being seedbeds of hypocrisy and expediency, and of being perpetuated only to maintain the status quo. They are seen to be the tools of the conservatives to brainwash people regarding home, morality, country, and economic systems. Persons who follow the traditional spiritual disciplines are thought to be interested only in keeping control and forcing nonconformists into neat little packages. There is only one reality and that is the reality of experience. How a person feels is the rule and guide in the search.

It is not strange that Oriental mysticism, Satan worship, witchcraft, astrology, black magic, voodooism, and spiritualism appeal to these persons who are in search of themselves as well as of friendly, intimate persons and forces outside of themselves.

Some of these persons go on to become Jesus freaks. Jesus the mystic is followed as the source and medium of the mystical experience. Certain experiences and teachings of Jesus become "scriptures" along with the teaching and leadership of others who are seen to be going in the same direction, saying the same thing. The pentecostal experience of speaking in tongues becomes a necessary part of the spiritual life. Communal living, love, sharing, helping are all carefully extracted from the teaching of Jesus. There are extreme attitudes even among the Jesus freaks. Some become fundamentalists and attempt to legislate pietism from the New Testament standards. Others are content to have an open attitude toward truth and experiences from sources outside the New Testament. Strange combinations of drug abuse, sacraments, and ethical living can result from this liberal approach of Jesus.

There is a great need for intimacy and identity. The impersonality of the home and community has driven people to search for fulfillment in the dimension of the Natural Child. Persons may not know whether they were baptized or confirmed, but they know their sign of zodiac and welcome as brothers and sisters those who are likewise designated.

The popularity of various types of sensitivity groups today shows a mass need to have intimacy. These groups have taken on some bizarre overtones from "touch and know sessions" to discussions in the nude. It is the Natural Child's way of saying, "I want to be intimate. I want to feel and know the truth. I want to have a feeling relationship with others. I want to be accepted even though I have imperfections. I want to love and be loved." It is not accidental that these groups have sprung up at a time when relationships in the established church are often cold and impersonal; where what you are and what you have to offer are considered to be more important than your personal relationships with others; where jamming people into preconceived molds is seen as necessary and desirable; where persons are made to feel "NOT OK." In the encounter groups, persons feel "OK." The philosophy of the encounter movement is "I'M OK—YOU'RE OK," a message that is of great significance to those who have never felt "OK" before. After all, the approach of Jesus is from the "I'M OK—YOU'RE OK" position.

To be able to understand rationally the philosophy and happenings in sensitivity groups is probably not possible. The Adult dimension is not a necessity for these groups. Truth is not conveyed through the mind but through the feelings of the "OK Child." To appreciate the attraction and satisfaction of having an intimate sharing of lives in an encounter group one must approach the group through the qualities of the Natural Child, a dimension that many older persons seem to be unable or unwilling to muster.

The traditional approach of organized religion has turned away more than just the young people. What comes across pulpit and pew sometimes is such a far cry from the life and teaching of Jesus, its founder, that even discerning older persons have to make a constant effort to remain in good standing with the church. Many people love Jesus and the church that bears his name, but they see the glaring contradiction between what is preached in the traditional church and what Jesus taught twenty centuries ago.

Of all the things that can be said of people today who are outside organized religion, one thing is not true: that they are atheists. In fact, some of them are closer to the spirit of Jesus than many who tithe of their income and go to worship several times during the week. The chapters on "Jesus Had a Liberated Child" and "The Early Church and the Liberated Child" make the point that what makes Jesus meaningful and pertinent today is that he had a liberated "OK" Natural Child.

One can discern how illiterate and ignorant people turn to superstitions and the mystical to fulfill the urge and effort of the Natural Child. If this generation is doing the same, it is because there is a basic need in a person, and the established church is not satisfying that need. Every religious tangent pursued by people today should be a reminder to the established church of its inability and inadequacy in meeting the needs of the Natural Child; consequently, people look here and there in hopes of stumbling across someone or something that *will* speak to their needs. Rather than being threatened by the competition, the established churches and denominations should hire a consulting firm to evaluate their methods and mission. It may cost a few dollars, but it would be greatly worth it.

EXPENSIVE TOYS

One of the attempts to liberate the Natural Child of grownups is through expensive toys. The difference between a man and a boy is in the cost of his "toys." America's showrooms have a magnificent assortment of equipment, fun machines, gadgets, often listed under the subject of sporting and recreational gear. Billions of dollars are spent every year to purchase this endless list of materials and additional billions are required to keep them operating.

It is the same motivation that causes an eight-year-old gleefully to examine the contents of a shop specializing in toys and the thirty-year-old man gleefully to visit the shops specializing in speed and sporting equipment, motorcycles, sports cars, sailboats, motor homes, speed boats, camping equipment, dune buggies, dragsters, hot rods, airplanes, lighter-than-air balloons, golf clubs, water skis, fishing rods, reels and artificial lures, campers, snow skis, basketballs, stereos or color televisions, sky-diving materials, skin-diving, antique car restoration, or gardening equipment. To be able to activate the little boy or girl in a person, even if it is for only a few brief moments, is thought to be something worth seeking.

Lest the above sound like negativism I note that this is not a crusade to stamp out fun for grown people. In the competitive, pressurized society in which we live a person needs some diversion and recreation. Every man needs a hobby or hobbies to give him some fulfillment as well as entertainment.

Somehow, though, there has developed a philosophy that in order to have fun you have to have the "right" equipment, equipment expensive not only to buy but also to maintain. The rate of annual depreciation is astronomical. The licensing, personal property taxes, and related equipment causes people to sink a huge amount of money in recreational boats and vehicles. To finance these expensive toys takes a serious bite out of sometimes strained budgets. Sometimes operating costs are so expensive the equipment stands unused in the driveway or garage, a pitiful sight to observe. Like a wild duck with a crippled wing is a cabin cruiser placed on blocks because the owner does not have the money to buy gasoline for the thirsty engine.

Watch an uptight, clock-conscious, deadline-bound executive liberate the child, go aboard his sailboat, hoist the sail, and head out to deep waters where the breezes blow strong. Watch the clergyman dash out of the office at a prearranged time, race his car to the golf course, grab his golf clubs, and literally run to the first tee shot, where there are no telephones or boards of deacons. Notice the housewife on Friday afternoon as she loads the camping trailer with food and water in anticipation of the husband's arrival and the launching out for a weekend of fun and frolic in the great out-of-doors. Observe the stockbroker who on coming home to his castle drops his coat, tie, and hang-ups as he heads for the family room and his HO model railroad, where he is the engineer as well as the owner. Watch the man and wife who have two hill-climbing motorcycles head for the wilderness and then "rev" up the cycles and cruise up and down the hills and explore some areas and make some trails where man has never been before.

There is a little boy or a little girl in each of us that longs for recognition and freedom. It is the same little boy or little girl that used to play "dress up" and "cowboys." The need to liberate the Child in grownups is as necessary as it is for children. To get away from responsibilities, problems, pressures, tensions, telephones, appointments, commitments, the calendar, the clock, and the image, it is so important for moderns to liberate the Child in order to keep from taking life so seriously and to find some pleasure and fulfillment. The only problem with the method is that some persons take on such an expensive liberation that they must "moonlight" to pay for the equipment.

There needs to be a liberation of the Child, in the air, on the water, under the water, on wheels, on the land. But the purpose is to let the Child enjoy life, which modern living seems to discourage.

To discover less expensive and burdensome ways to liberate the Natural Child would be more fulfilling and fun. A ten-foot rowboat with a five-horsepower outboard engine that is free of a mortgage is much to be desired over a recreational vehicle that has been purchased with payments extending over ten years.

Free your Child! Get some recreational equipment; your little boy or girl inside you wants to be liberated so much. But watch the obligations of your liberation.

EPICUREAN PLEASURES

The philosophy of life and the motivation for daily living for many persons in this decade is the spirit of the Greek philosopher Epicurus, who lived several centuries before the birth of Christ. The goal for men, according to him, is living a life of pleasure by finding fulfillment in sensuous outlets. Though the founder of this school of living believed there should be temperance and restraints, modern advocates of the life of pleasure seem to believe in pulling out all the stops, having large appetites for pleasure to the point of gluttony and excess.

The purpose of food and drink is to supply the nourishment and fluids for a healthy body and mind, measurable in terms of calories. When the body receives more calories than it can effectively oxidize, it stores the surplus in various lumps and rolls about the body. This added weight handicaps the victim by limiting his activities, shortening his life, and putting a strain on his body, particularly the heart and circulatory system. Overweight is caused by the Child dimension being in control. The motivation to overindulgence may come from either the Adapted Child, who learned at an early age to get brownie stamps for stuffing himself with food, or from the Natural Child who finds great pleasure in eating. To complicate matters, appetizing food is usually loaded with calories, a situation which prompts the person to have even seconds and thirds and sometimes more.

It is one thing to be a gourmet eater and quite another to be a glutton. A gourmet appreciates good food in regard to quality and flavor. A glutton has a voracious appetite and stuffs himself with huge quantities of food. Both the gourmet and the glutton are in the Natural Child dimension and find enjoyment in eating and drinking. The gourmet, however, has the Adult dimension supervising his gastronomic intake and his choice of menu; the glutton has no motivation to limit the pleasure he discovers with his fork.

An important insight is that when a person eats his food, he is usually in the dimension of the Child. It is important that the Adult supervise mealtime and snacktime, so that a balanced diet is eaten and the temptations to excess are stifled. Obesity has a number of emotional and physical causes. In addition to earning brownie stamps for forced feeding, a person may eat excessively, not only as an escape and for pleasure, but to punish someone. A heavy man or woman may have gotten that way just to get even with the mate for some real or imagined injustice.

Eating or drinking excessively is done in the dimension of the Child. The motivation to temperance and/or dieting comes from the dimension of Adult (the scale says you are getting overweight) or the Parent (you are just too fat). When the Adult is in control a careful planning of the quality and quantity of food is made. There is only one drawback: the Child that enjoys eating and satisfying his pleasure may be able to silence the inputs of the Parent or the Adult. What dimension is a person in when he raids the refrigerator or freezer? What dimension is he in when he has a "midnight snack?" What dimension is he in when he has an extra large dessert or a second helping of something that tastes really good? The answer, of course, is the Child.

Moderns have discovered how to liberate the Child. They do it in the kitchen or dining room. But frequently the Child is liberated at the expense of the Adult. By the way, when a person becomes overweight it protrudes in all three dimensions. This really upsets the Parent and the Adult dimensions, causing them to wrest control from the Child and go on a diet.

Moderns find pleasure in many places, and when they do so they liberate the Child. Watching spectator sports either at the stadium or on television is an excellent place to hear the language and see the features of the Natural Child. Religious leaders have long lamented that they are unable to compete with sporting events, whether they be on the level of little league, junior high and high schools, college or professional athletics. Perhaps if they would take the time to evaluate what dimension people take to sporting events and what dimension the clergy normally insist that people bring to church, they would realize that spectator sports appeal to the Natural or "OK CHILD" but the traditional approach for religious services is for the people to come in the Adapted or "NOT OK CHILD."

Team spirit and team support find expression in the dimension of the Natural Child. Try to justify logically paying ten or more dollars to sit in the cold for three hours while twenty-two men try to move a football around on a muddy field. It is not uncommon that when the Natural Child's appetite is whetted for enjoying a certain game he may pay a hundred dollars or more for a ticket, a move hardly justifiable in the dimension of the Adult.

Epicurean pleasures can be sought in many places from mink-lined toilet seats to automatic bed warmers. The pleasures derived from luxurious living appeal to the Natural Child who looks for bigger, more vivid, and more frequent enjoyment of sensational living. When the

Child is liberated so he can enjoy the benefits of quality living, he gets the benefit of the pleasure itself plus the pleasure of talking about it to his friends. But as with all pleasures in life enjoyed by the Natural Child, unless there is Adult supervision sensations which were once pleasurable become monsters bringing havoc and waste and unhappiness.

A WORLD OF FANTASY

America is known for "make-believe." Not only at Christmas but on birthdays and anniversaries it is believed that there is surprise and mystery always just around the corner. A chicken in every pot; a car in every garage; a gift in every box. The fantasylands of the country are all constructed for children, but what does it matter if the children are fifty years old?

On each coast now there is a fantasyland, places planned just to appeal to the Natural Child of people. The circus is nearly dead but fantasyland goes on forever. The personification of bears, pigs, mice, cats, birds, elephants who communicate and have transactions—that is the imagery of this generation. These challenging figures are as real as the person living next door or Aunt Minnie or Uncle Bill. Everyone knows that mice can talk and that roadrunners are smarter than coyotes. Everyone knows what a bear sounds like when he talks (for he has heard Smokey the Bear talk many times), and everyone knows that crickets have personal names like Jimminy Cricket.

The world of fantasy and make-believe appeals to the Natural Child of persons of all ages. No one has to teach another that riding on a merry-go-round is fun, a ferris wheel is exciting, a sliding board or swings are enjoyable. Built into each person is the ability to liberate the Child and experience enjoyment on the playground and in the amusement park. It is the Natural Child that finds pleasure in a roller coaster, monkey bars, ride-em and dodge'em, a cartoon show, puppets, dancing, spin the bottle, playing post office, bobbing for apples, ghost stories, Halloween dress-up, lodge and club initiation, fireworks, water skiing, cotton candy, baseball and football games, bicycle-riding, jumping rope, hopscotch, flirting, teasing, tickling, joking, laughing, singing, a band concert, rock and roll, bowling, playing tag, going fast, pinball machines, ice cream, soda pop, peanuts and popcorn, candy bars and chewing gum, bubble gum, coloring and painting pictures, hobbies, climbing trees, swimming, skating, playing a harmonica, eating, drinking, sleeping, rodeos, motorcycles, inventing, curiosity, wonder, kite-flying, sail-boating, excitement, crying, hoping, wishing, believing, optimism, happiness, freedom, fishing, bird-watching, enjoyment of pets, magic, juggling, gymnastics, picnics, lemonade, birthday cakes, gifts, Christmas trees, movie theaters, stuffed animals, games, colored paper, ribbons, record players, television, stereo equipment, dreaming, day-dreaming, make believe, imagination, and fantasy. These are all enjoyed by the Child in persons, whether they be old or young. Persons who have the Adult in control and who know the motivation of the Natural Child have the potential insight to attract interest and make money by building concessions that appeal to the Natural Child.

The fantasy that many used to dream about in the dimension of the Natural Child was running away from home (and responsibilities) and joining the circus. Even to feed and water the elephants would be fun in a fun world. Today the whole family runs away from the dull and routine and finds expression and relief in the liberation of the Child in the world of fantasy.

It is not unusual to see a middle-aged man or woman who has everything going for him—education, status, financial security, and reputation—throw up the traces and run away to begin a new life. Old relationships are abandoned and substitutes accepted. A wife or husband of thirty years duration is divorced, the job is quit, the retirement program abandoned, the predictable becomes unpredictable. This is the Natural Child having a fling without Adult or Parent supervision. You can never understand the change in a person's approach by examining the facts and the data; you must look at the situation through the qualities of the Natural Child if you want to feel what this person is feeling and hence his motivation. When this happens to a friend or relative a person first goes through a period of shock. When one tries to understand using the Parent (what's right or wrong) or the Adult (what's logical) one comes up with a big question mark. There is no *rational* explanation for this 180° shift in personality. If any light is to be shed on the subject the evaluator must use the same dimension to evaluate the situation as the original person used when he made the break with the traditional; that is, the Natural Child. The only explanation is that the person is living in a world of fantasy and that feelings are now more important than facts. This is a liberation of the Child that has been so unhappy for so many years that a drastic effort must be made to find maximum happiness immediately to make up for all the pleasure that has been missed. Chances for satisfying living are quickly sifting through the hour glass of life. A desperate situation requires desperate action. There is little or no concern what people may think when the Natural Child is calling the shots and is unswerved in the decisions by either the Parent or the Adult.

The enjoyment and appreciation of music is a suitable example of what appeals to Natural Child, the Adult, the Parent, or the Adapted Child. The traditional, the accepted, historical, the conservative can be appreciated by those who find that organization, dependability, analysis, predictability, specialization, artistry, discipline, and dedication are important. When you have to give a course in music appreciation and teach people how and what to enjoy in music, you may have already ruined their ability to discover what brings musical pleasure to them. Like the parables told by Jesus, if you have to ask what they mean you have already limited your ability to appreciate and understand them. For parables and music appreciation must come in the dimension of the Natural Child, with the Adult giving only supervision.

A rock group of five performers with questionable musical training may draw a larger crowd and appeal to more persons than musicians trained by many years of discipline and study who brilliantly perform a difficult symphonic program. Whether the music is in tune, whether it has permanence, whether it can be analyzed and scored—these are of little or no significance to those who like what they hear and what they hear, they like. When others in the dimension of the Parent or the Adult attempt to evaluate modern expressive music they throw up their hands, finding it monotonous, out of tune; the lyrics do not make sense, it is too loud and may even be vulgar. Only when the Natural Child listens to music can the music be enjoyed. The Natural Child knows what he likes to hear. He will find it difficult to share these strong feelings with others who are hung up on either the Parent or Adult dimension. He will be able to rap for hours about music with those who are in the dimension of the Natural Child. There is a difference between music appreciation and music enjoyment. The ability to liberate the Child to enjoy music has little to do with chronological age.

In the world of fantasy where sights and sounds are vivid, where colors and feelings are brilliant, where imagination and wonder are present, where make believe and thrills are interwoven, where happiness and pleasure are norms, there is the dimension that is enjoyed in the liberation of the Child. Logical explanations may be made to rationalize driving two thousand miles to find a fantasyland but they will be unconvincing unless the Natural Child is in control of the hearer. One may say, "We are making the trip for our children," but a more accurate statement would be, "The Natural Child of the whole family is anxious to experience the make-believe wonders of fantasyland. Won't it be fun?" Fantasyland is found wherever the Natural Child wants to go, where he can find pleasure and fun and happiness. The little boy or little girl in each of us still loves the taste of cotton candy, popcorn balls, and glazed apples. Even some odors can liberate the Child. You could be blindfolded and still liberate the Child by being led past a bakery, through the aisles of a ten-cent store, through the sidewalks of a zoo, down the midway of the carnival. You could also liberate the Child through the sense of sight, touch, taste, and hearing, for the Child is the sensuous part of a person and loves to explore old and new ways to be liberated.

Modern attempts to liberate the Child involve chemicals, sex, religious tangents, expensive toys, epicurean pleasures, and fantasylands. The Child wants and needs to be liberated but disastrous results will come unless there is Adult supervision. Free your Child. Let out the little boy or little girl in you to enjoy the sights, sounds, colors, tastes, smells, and touches of life. Only have the Adult dimension be present to chaperon the enjoyment of the Child.

11

Liberating the Child
in the Home

One of the most frequently asked questions in a counseling session where a husband and wife have begun to grasp the method of Transactional Analysis is, "What does all this mean as far as raising our children is concerned?" To put it another way, "How can we train our children to be productive and happy so that they may find fulfillment in life?" This is a searching and important question and should be faced by mothers and fathers who not only want to share helpful insights and tools with their offspring, but also want them to find happiness in the process.

It must be recognized that a person cannot give what he has not known himself. Persons can only share what they have experienced. For this reason it is so important for the grownups to set their own house in order before they can hope to share effective handles and insights with their children. Hypocrisy and role-playing on the part of mothers and fathers is usually discovered by their children. An attempt to project an image as father or mother will be seen through by the whole family. Children will soon spot the conflict between what a mother or father "says" and what he "does."

If Transactional Analysis cannot be effectively applied in the home then it is worthless to try to master the technique. Those persons, however, who have used it to gain insights in their relationships have found that the application in the home, by all members of the family, to be infinite and satisfying. Fortunate are the children who have mothers and fathers motivated to use this method of evaluating relationships, who seek the goal of putting the Adult in control to process data and make decisions; to evaluate the inputs of the Parent; to shut the Parent off when it is inappropriate, and to liberate the Natural Child and supervise his conduct.

The most appropriate life-style for the home is "I'M OK—YOU'RE OK." This philosophy of life needs to undergird all family relationships. Even in potential life and injury situations, when the Parent must have strong confrontations with the Adapted Child, the underlying life-style should be "OK-ness." Mothers and fathers need to establish rules and enforce them from an "I'M OK—YOU'RE OK" position. Family life, however, is not always democratic. Since the mother and father are older than the children, and it is hoped wiser, they must sometimes make decisions on behalf of the children and be willing to assume the responsibility for these decisions. Times of immunization, trips to the physician and dentist, a balanced diet, attendance at school, homework completion are a few of these instances. If religion is a meaningful experience for father and mother, then this resource should be shared with the children who may later choose to go to another church or may even choose not to go at all.

Family members need to see the uniqueness of the makeup and personality of each, that people are of great value and have infinite potential, that the past can be used to gain an occasional insight, but that the present and the future are the important elements of time. Persons in the family need to make choices on the basis of facts and be willing to assume the responsibility for the consequences of their choices. The home should be the place where an individual can be treated as a valuable resource and asset, and where the person is accepted, not for some projected image, but just because he is a person. As one family member has admirably said, "Home is where you can scratch yourself, no matter where you itch."

There is a place for rules and standards in the home. To protect property rights and maintain human dignity for all persons in the home, there have to be guidelines. Respect for the laws of the land and moral conduct are best taught where people relate to one another, not by legalistic dictation, but by loving relationships. The home is an ideal environment for learning these important insights about human relations.

It is difficult for a father or mother to think of their offspring as having three dimensions. When the children are young, it is easy for the seniors to relate to the juniors as Parent-Adapted Child. The children are so dependent upon the leadership and support of the father and mother they must be told when to do things and how to do them. They must be supervised and protected. Something as simple as tying shoes and taking a bath must be specifically taught by those who know the technique. The older persons expect to tell and the youngsters expect to be told. There are times when the Parent-Adapted Child relation is appropriate, especially when danger is present or anticipated. "Do this!" "Don't do that!" "Get away from the fire!" "Don't touch that wire!" "Don't climb that shaky wall!" "Don't go into the street!" "Don't touch that car door handle!" "Don't play with those matches!" "Don't go near that ledge!" "Don't touch the gun!" There are possibilities of injury in these situations and they deserve the Parent-Adapted Child approach. But it is a shame when the only way a father can deal with his children is through this method. It would be detrimental to a little one's growth and development to have the older person always standing over him dictating the proper course of action, especially if the same admonitions were used regarding a glass of milk as playing in the street.

A two-year-old has the dimensions of Parent, Adult, and Child and can relate to others in each of these dimensions. To communicate about the danger of the street the older person should approach the subject Adult-Adult. "Billy, to go in the street is a dangerous thing to do. Cars drive in the street. Sometimes they cannot see little people who run into the street. Children can be hit by a car and hurt. Remember what happened to Jimmy's puppy that got hit by the car? This can even happen to little people." The father then says, "And if I ever see you in the street I will spank you!" This is Parent-Adapted Child. Looking out the window one day the father sees Billy standing in the center of the street. If the father is worth his salt he will go out, grab Billy, take him to the sidewalk and do what he promised to do. However, the Adult of the father supervises the administering of discipline, and gives only enough spanks to make the point. It would be unfortunate if Billy's Dad spanked Billy for spilling his milk at the table as well as standing in the street. Spanking should be reserved for life and injury situations.

As Billy grows older, it is hoped his Dad more and more uses the Adult-Adult method of communication, which includes discipline and punishment. To spank a teenager may bring some satisfaction to the father, but it brings out some feelings of anger in the son. For a father to spank his teenage daughter may arouse some inappropriate feelings in both the father and the daughter.

One of the weaknesses of the Parent-Adapted Child relationship is that it teaches the little ones to begin saving brownie stamps at an early age. Some children are professional brownie stamp savers by the time they start to school. They do anything to get the approval of the Parent, and hence, brownie stamps. Mothers and Fathers who know the value of brownie stamps are likely to teach this diligently to their offspring. There is a relationship between how many stamps are earned by the little ones and the degree that the Parent loves them. Lots of stamps means lots of love and acceptance; carelessness in obedience may produce feelings of rejection and not being loved. The Parent really says to the Adapted Child, "If you do this or that I will give you your reward." Not only is there a brownie stamp involved but some stroking as well.

One of the most pathologic of mother-children relations was described by a mother. "I play a game with my children when their father is not around. I ask them to do something, and to get it done I sit on the floor and fake crying. Finally the children notice me and ask what is wrong. I tell them if they do this or that, Mommy will stop crying." They hurriedly do what Mommy has asked, just to get Mommy to stop crying. What would you believe she is programing her children to do when they also are married and have a family? They will believe that this is the "right" way for a mother to get work done around the house! Imagine what must go on in the home between wife and husband, if the wife must be such a faker to get her strokes! One wonders what kind of a home she was from and how other members of the family got their stroking.

Children learn to play house just as they observe Mom and Dad doing. Their ability to figure out logically what is happening will probably not take place until after their Parent dimension is already formed. The authoritarian inputs are carefully recorded by the little person for future reference and use. All the data recorded in the Parent dimension are accepted as fact, whether true, half-true, or completely false. What a healthy home it is when Mom and Dad carefully control the dimension of their Parent with the data processing of the Adult, so that when they come through as Parent it is appropriate, true, and necessary.

The one dimension that is often lacking between husband and wife is the Natural Child. When these two have an intimate relationship going on at gut level, when their relationship is strong enough to weather some confrontation and differences of opinion, when they do not have to perform or play a role, or project some sort of an image, when they can be themselves and be loved as themselves, with imperfections and hang-ups as well as some strong qualities, then the situation might be comfortable enough for them to liberate the Natural Child. Is it not a shame that, when young people relate to each other, too often it is only during the courtship period that they love to be together, doing things together, relating together, talking together? Whole evenings could be spent just talking about aspirations, expectations, and interests. But some couples spoil the relationship by getting married, for marriage seems to be the most disastrous wet blanket that can be thrown upon a beautiful relationship!

During courtship shared ideas and things in common are important facts to be considered. Weaknesses, imperfections, social consciousness, shortcomings, hang-ups, prejudices, shortsightedness, ignorance, and lack of finesse, are often ignored or minimized. But after a year of marriage the couple that was so compatible (i.e., congenial, capable of existing together, in harmony with each other, having rapport, being in step, having accord, having a common purpose and spirit, agreeing, comformable, reconcilable, congruous) are now finding that they have more in contradiction than they do in common. Were it not for the verification of the model for marriage ("all our friends are as unhappy as we") these couples would run, not walk, to the nearest legal counsel and divorce court to terminate the relationship.

"I want a girl just like the girl that married dear ole Dad."

The only problem is that Dad got her and she was a collector's item; one of a kind. The man and the woman both complacently say, "I'll have to be satisfied with what I got." "I made my bed, now I will have to lie in it." "I'll just grit my teeth and bear what I must bear." "Life is not a bed of roses." These are good statements for one who is interested in maintaining a martyr image, and there are many persons in a marriage and family relationship who have a martyr complex. But what poorer place to project this image than in a home where little children grow into maturity, building their lives on what they see.

Happy are the children who are fortunate enough to be born in a home where the mother and father know how to play. This is the real liberation of the Natural Child if it is supervised by the Adult. This environment is the most helpful and happy seedbed for growth, maturity, and happiness for little persons to be surrounded by and to develop in, growing up in the "liberation of the Child." The kind of play is not a father who is motivated to take his sons fishing because he read a book on the subject. It is not the mother who wants to be buddy-buddy with her daughters and attempts to talk, dress, and act like a teenager.

It is the responsibility of both husband and wife to relate in a loving and open way to each other. When children see Dad give Mom a pat on the backside, or a kiss on the cheek, they are assured that these two "ding-a-lings" like to be near each other. One of the nicest of compliments is to be labeled as a "ding-a-ling," for this shows the dimension of the Natural Child. The term dingbat implies a Parent-Adapted Child approach—"I'M OK—YOU'RE NOT OK." The healthy approach is "I'M OK—YOU'RE OK," or "I'm a ding-a-ling and I like being with ding-a-lings. They are my kind of people."

A "ding-a-ling" does not take life too seriously. He knows how to relax, take it easy, enjoy life. He is in the "OK" dimension, and knows how to relate with others in this same dimension.

Families who "play" together stay together. To be able to liberate the Natural Child under Adult supervision is one of the most meaningful relationships to have in the home. The dimension that is lacking in most families is the ability to "play" together, to enjoy each other, to relax with each other, to accept each other, to have fun with each other. This does not mean that Mom or Dad plays children's games and pretends to lose in competition with them (the children know when you stack the cards in their favor). It is the ability to be a person and be accepted as a person with no axe to grind and no image to project. The brownie stamp book needs to be ceremonially put in its trash can! "Down with brownie stamps!" "Patronize only the places that assure you that they don't give brownie stamps!" "Keep brownie stamps out of the home!" "Let your life be free of brownie stamps!" "Do something for someone just because you love him!" "Savers of brownie stamps, Revolt!" "Burn the brownie stamps!" These would all make admirable slogans and the motivation to stamp out brownie stamps once and for all.

Would it not be a beautiful sight to see children loved and stroked not because of obedience and fidelity, but because they are of great value and worth? Would it not be a glowing insight into life if brothers could relate to sisters, not by what they should do for each other or what they have done, but just because they are beloved as family members? Would it not be great if husbands and wives could experience a resurrection of the courting relationship where the optimism, enthusiasm, and expectancy in the eyes of both the man and the woman could be recaptured and relived in a marriage relationship? Is it possible for this generation to "free the Child," in the husband/father, wife/mother, girl/daughter, boy/son? This liberation could take place through the Adult, who looks at the facts, makes responsible decisions, turns off the Parent when its inputs are inappropriate, and liberates the Child while supervising his antics. Child liberation is the watchword and the goal.

If it is not possible to have a "liberation of the Child" in the home then the whole liberation movement is gone astray. The home is the nucleus of the community. The community is the temperature of the nation. The nation is the condition of the world. The world is the hope of humanity. Humanity is the most valuable and meaningful asset of the universe, for God has for decades, centuries, and eons of time been trying to communicate with humans. "Free your Child." Let him live again in the security and love of being accepted—not for an image or a player's role, but for being himself; "Free your Child!" This is the most worthy and the most challenging of motivations. "Free your Child!"

A part of "growing up" is "growing away" from the necessity of the Parent-Adapted Child relationship. Being independent; able to deal with facts and make responsible decisions, able to assume the consequences of the decisions, to control the Parent inputs and to liberate and supervise the Natural Child—all these are signs that the Adult dimension is healthy and functioning. This should be the goal of mothers and fathers who are concerned about their offspring.

Many older persons are visibly shaken when they realize for the first time that the Parent dimension in their children is really themselves and that this authority dimension will be a part of their offspring the rest of their lives. That you will become incarnated in your children is a sobering thought, especially when the input has been set in concrete by the time children are six years old and your children have all passed this age. It is consistently true that when the mothers and fathers learn the method of Transactional Analysis they have a strong desire to re-rear their children, only this time to use these benefits in getting handles on family relationships. Alas, the Parent dimension is already probably conditioned and if it is ever modified it has to come from a deliberate and painful effort on the part of the offspring, as new and more appropriate authority inputs are rationally and logically encountered and evaluated.

What mothers and fathers need to come to terms with and to share with their children is the ability to turn off the Parent dimension when it is not consistent with the facts and when it causes more damage than good. This is a terribly threatening thought for some mothers and fathers. To teach their children to turn "themselves" (the Parent dimension) off when it is inappropriate is a serious blow to the image that some mothers and fathers hold of themselves. For everything that they have felt was important in life, including what is morally right and wrong; what is proper and necessary; the basis of prejudice, status, and success; economics, patriotism, politics, and religion—these all have come through Parent-Adapted Child and become a part of the Parent dimension of the children. To begin questioning the "facts" in these "sacred" areas is like questioning the existence of God, the value of motherhood, the significance of the American flag, or the necessity of democracy.

Young couples who have the motivation to relate in marriage and rear their children using these insights of Transactional Analysis are in a wonderful position to encourage maturity and growth, and develop potential, resulting in fulfilling experiences for themselves and their families. Having the Adult in control permits the couple to make responsible decisions, deal with the facts, use the authority dimension when it is helpful but turn it off when it is a hindrance; to liberate the "OK CHILD" in the home is a beautiful and fulfilling dimension of living. This quality of life is within reach of anyone motivated to make the effort to put the Adult in control.

The modern home is so fragmented and undercut by competitive forces which demand time and effort that rarely is the whole family ever together at any given moment. Home today is more of a combined service station, transportation terminal, laundromat, telephone answering service, cafeteria, and motel than it is an integrated family unit. It is functional but not fulfilling. The real spirit of the family has been replaced by an impersonal, selfish attitude of "What's in it for me?" There is little difference today between a religious and a nonreligious family. Both have been caught up in the same merry-go-round existence and few persons are looking for the master switch that turns it off. It is suggested that because the home has lost its appeal the members of the family must look outside the home for fulfillment. When families no longer play together, organized little leagues must be formed to program the time. Then the fathers and mothers must provide leadership and bus service to and from the "professional" games. It is regrettable that boys as young as eight years old are already becoming specialists in local sporting contests. These games are rarely played for fun; they are played to win. Batting averages and yards gained by rushing are important statistics for these youngsters. You can even earn brownie stamps on the football and baseball field. Church-sponsored teams also encourage the collection of brownie stamps.

Some families are able to hang together only *because* of this impersonal nature of the home. If people were thrown together too much, life would be even more boring or painful. If this present way of life and family living were satisfying and fulfilling, if it encouraged the participants to prepare for the future and become mature, responsible persons, then one might ignore some of the weaknesses and look for the future gratifications. But impersonal family living is a cop-out for the fathers and mothers who have nothing better to offer in its place.

What is needed in the home today is a "Child Liberation Movement." What is meant by this is a liberation of the Natural or "OK CHILD" so that life could once again be meaningful and fulfilling, so that all family members be recognized as important assets and resources, so that the Adult be encouraged to motivate the Adapted Child to stop collecting brownie stamps, and so that the Parent be evaluated and shut up when it is inappropriate.

PART **IV**
Epilog

12

Building on
a Sure Foundation

Traditionally, there has been much discussion as to whether there is life after death. Many theories and positions have been expounded to prove or disprove the thesis of life after death. Life after death is a very important and fascinating study and goal. This book, however, is concerned as to whether there is life *before* death; or, to put it another way, whether living can be more than just existing. Whatever the number of years that a person lives, is it not a shame that so few persons really find fulfillment and happiness?

For many persons life is drab, monotonous, and without meaning. Days run into weeks and months and years. The television set may become the baby sitter for the old and young alike, with its rerun programs and idiotic commercials structuring the hours of the day and night. The traditional church, with the traditional prayers, the traditional scripture lessons, the traditional sermons, the traditional hymns, the traditional rituals on the traditional holy days, with the traditional ho-hum response, by the traditional people in the pulpit and pews—all contribute to the traditional deterioration of the Christian faith and its traditional irrelevance for modern man.

I seriously doubt that a person who is unable to find life before death will ever find it after death. I question whether a person who does not know the love of God in this life would ever recognize it in the afterlife. I suspect that a person who cannot recognize his "brother or

sister" now will be unable to know family relationships later. I find it
unbelievable that a person who cannot love the people he has met and
known on earth will ever be able to love strangers in heaven. I think it is
preposterous that an uptight, self-righteous snob here and now will be
able to relax for eternity with those outside his own little clique. I feel it
is improbable that one who has not known the fullness of joy in the flesh
will ever know joy in the spirit.

Life in this world is not some proving ground to earn brownie
stamps for the future; it is the gift of God offered to those who can
muster the dimension of personality to desire and recognize it. The
kingdom of heaven is in our midst, as Jesus so beautifully states it. His
whole approach to life and living was based upon the reality of the love
of God and man. His verbal and nonverbal teaching about fulfillment in
this life provides the direction and motivation for mortals who are able
to respond to his love. Jesus hewed out the dimensions and designs of a
beautiful life relationship of such mortals with each other and with God.
The method of Transactional Analysis gives the working tools and
blueprints for evaluating relationships, including those with God. The
Christian faith as lived and taught by Jesus shows the quality of life that
is offered to any who can free the Natural Child by the Adult. The nuts
and bolts of the Christian faith concern relationships, and relationships
are the nitty-gritty of Transactional Analysis.

Personality comes in three dimensions. Each dimension is helpful if
it is appropriate for the transaction. The dimension of man or God that
permits responsibility in goal-setting, decision-making, and interpersonal relationships is the Adult or reason. This facet of personality gives
direction by confrontation with the data of reality, as well as evaluating
and channeling the authority of the Parent. But real living is not found
until the Natural or "OK CHILD" is liberated and supervised by the
Adult. The Natural Child is the dimension that responds to the Natural
Child dimension (Holy Spirit) of God, and then reflects this loving
relationship with others who can also liberate their "OK CHILD."
Grace is the beautiful concern of God for man. Jesus makes grace a
reality, and Transactional Analysis provides the handles for recognizing
and receiving it. The fulfillment of life is experienced in the dimension
of the liberated Child supervised by the Adult.

Jesus is the quarterback of the team owned by God who invites
persons in the dimension of the Natural Child to enjoy the game of life.
Transactional Analysis is the strategy drawn on the chalkboard to
diagnose the plays and evaluate the resulting scrimmage. There may be

enjoyment in watching others in the encounter, but the Christian faith is not a spectator sport. The real joy comes from the encounters on the field, both in the intimacy of the team members, and in the shared joy of victory. This parable of life can be studied and evaluated by the reason, but like the parables of Jesus it is "understood" only by the Child.

Eternal life begins now or it will not begin at all. Life in this world is meant to be more than just counting the days and enumerating the accomplishments. There must be fulfillment beyond just doing what is logical or legal. Jesus has shown the quality of life that is within the grasp of every person. His primary purpose was to share his joy with those who could receive it, so that other persons could be brimful of this beautiful gift of God. Joy does not come through study or through directives, but through taking the leap of faith in the dimension of the Natural Child.

"Free the Child in you" and take an adventure into joyful living.

Bibliography

The Amplified Bible. Grand Rapids, Mich.: Zondervan, 1965.

The Interpreter's Bible (in twelve volumes). Nashville: Abingdon Press, 1951.

The Interpreter's Dictionary of the Bible (in four volumes). Nashville: Abingdon Press, 1962.

Berne, Eric. *Games People Play.* New York: Grove Press, 1964.

———. *Principles of Group Treatment.* New York: Oxford University Press, 1966; New York: Grove Press, 1969.

———. *Sex in Human Loving.* New York: Simon and Schuster, 1970.

———. *The Structure and Dynamics of Organizations and Groups.* New York: Grove Press, 1963.

———. *Transactional Analysis in Psychotherapy.* New York: Grove Press, 1961.

———. *What Do You Say After You Say Hello?* New York: Grove Press, 1972.

Bontrager, John. *Sea Rations.* Nashville: Upper Room Press, 1964.

Davis, John D. and Gehman, Henry S. *The Westminster Dictionary of the Bible.* Philadelphia: Westminster Press, 1944.

Fast, Julius. *Body Language.* New York: M. Evans & Co., 1970; New York: Pocket Books, 1971.

Ferm, Vergilius. *An Encyclopedia of Religion.* New York: Philosophical Library, 1945.

Harris, Thomas. *I'm OK—You're OK.* New York: Harper & Row, 1967.

James, Muriel and Jongeward, Dorothy. *Born to Win.* Reading, Mass.: Addison-Wesley Publishing Co., 1971.

Revised Standard Version of the Bible. New York: Thomas Nelson & Sons, 1946.

Steiner, Claude. *Games Alcoholics Play.* New York: Grove Press, 1971.

About the Author

John K. Bontrager is an ordained minister of the United Church of Christ. He is a captain in the Chaplain Corps of the U.S. Navy and has served in a variety of assignments in both the military and civilian ministry. Presently he is stationed at the Submarine Medical Center, Submarine Base, Groton, Connecticut, where he works as a member of the human relations team with the medical center staff psychiatrists, medical doctors, nurses, corpsmen, and members of the clergy.

Chaplain Bontrager is a graduate of Heidelberg College, Tiffin, Ohio, A.B., and the Graduate School of Theology, Oberlin College, Oberlin, Ohio, B.D. He holds the degree of Master of Divinity from Vanderbilt School of Theology, Nashville, Tennessee.

He has attended schools and seminars sponsored by the U.S. Navy Chaplain Corps including a counseling course at Berkeley, California, under the direction of the Pacific School of Religion in 1965, and the Senior Chaplain Advanced Course at Newport, Rhode Island, in 1970. He has served as President of Clergy Associations in Ohio and Connecticut. He was a member of the board of directors that established a mental health center for the three counties of Holmes, Wayne, and Medina in Ohio. After being ordained in 1952, Mr. Bontrager took his first pastoral assignment at the Millersburg-Glenmont Charge of the Evangelical and Reformed Church, which included St. John's UCC, Millersburg, and St. John's UCC, Glenmont, Ohio. In 1955 he was commissioned as a lieutenant (jg) in the Regular Navy Chaplain Corps where he has served aboard destroyers, an amphibious assault ship, and took overseas duties with the Marines, Seabees, and Coast Guard, as well as various U.S. continental assignments.

A veteran of World War II as an enlisted man, Chaplain Bontrager has served for twenty-one years of active-duty military service including assignments to Vietnam. Formerly a professional musician, he has used his talent to encourage persons to find fulfillment in music, as well as religion, and has organized and directed various musical groups. Two combos, "The Westwinds" and "The J P 5's," received national publicity for their musical programs and concerts in the combat area during the years 1967–68 when professional civilian groups were unable to tour the Southeast Asian combat area. He holds decorations and awards for distinguished service in the military and civilian ministry including the Navy Commendation Medal with the Combat V Device, Combat Action Ribbon, three awards of the Meritorious Unit Commendation, U.S. Coast Guard Good Conduct Medal, American Campaign Medal, World War II Victory Medal, China Service Medal (extended), National Defense Service Medal, Vietnam Service Medal (6 awards), Vietnam Cross of Galantry with Wreath, and Vietnam National Defense Medal with Device.